T0311820

Cambridge Elements ≡

Elements in Politics and Society in Southeast Asia
edited by
Edward Aspinall
Australian National University
Meredith L. Weiss
University at Albany, SUNY

SEXUALITY AND GENDER DIVERSITY RIGHTS IN SOUTHEAST ASIA

Anthony J. Langlois
Flinders University

CAMBRIDGE
UNIVERSITY PRESS

CAMBRIDGE
UNIVERSITY PRESS

University Printing House, Cambridge CB2 8BS, United Kingdom

One Liberty Plaza, 20th Floor, New York, NY 10006, USA

477 Williamstown Road, Port Melbourne, VIC 3207, Australia

314–321, 3rd Floor, Plot 3, Splendor Forum, Jasola District Centre, New Delhi – 110025, India

103 Penang Road, #05–06/07, Visioncrest Commercial, Singapore 238467

Cambridge University Press is part of the University of Cambridge.

It furthers the University's mission by disseminating knowledge in the pursuit of education, learning, and research at the highest international levels of excellence.

www.cambridge.org
Information on this title: www.cambridge.org/9781108927819
DOI: 10.1017/9781108933216

© Anthony J. Langlois 2022

First published 2022

A catalogue record for this publication is available from the British Library.

ISBN 978-1-108-92781-9 Paperback
ISSN 2515-2998 (online)
ISSN 2515-298X (print)

Sexuality and Gender Diversity Rights in Southeast Asia

Elements in Politics and Society in Southeast Asia

DOI: 10.1017/9781108933216
First published online: May 2022

Anthony J. Langlois
Flinders University

Author for correspondence: Anthony J. Langlois,
anthony.langlois@flinders.edu.au

Abstract: Sexuality and gender diversity rights in Southeast Asia are deeply controversial and vigorously contested. Debate and protest have been accompanied by both legislative reform and discriminatory violence. These contradictory dynamics are occurring at a time when the international human rights regime has explicitly incorporated a focus on the prevention of violence and discrimination in relation to sexuality and gender diversity. This Element focusses on the need for such rights. This Element explores the burgeoning of civil society organisations engaged in an emancipatory politics inclusive of sexuality and gender diversity, utilising rights politics as a platform for visibility, contestation and mobilisation. The author focusses on the articulation of political struggle through a shared set of rights claims, which in turn relates to shared experiences of violence and discrimination, and a visceral demand and hope for change.

This Element also has a video abstract: www.cambridge.org/langlois_abstract

Keywords: human rights, sexuality, gender, Southeast Asia, political participation

ISBNs: 9781108927819 (PB), 9781108933216 (OC)
ISSNs: 2515-2998 (online), 2515-298X (print)

Contents

Across the ASEAN region, LGBTIQ persons are either treated as second class citizens, criminals, are seen as deviants, and in some cases are not even recognised as human beings. We are made to lead dual lives and be ashamed of ourselves for who we are. We are subjected to name calling, condemnation, taunts, reparative treatments and other inhumane abuses. Discrimination and violence come not only from our families, friends, communities, and employers but also from state institution such as state actors, especially police and religious officers. Even in the face of discrimination and violence, the governments refuse to protect our basic human rights.

ASEAN SOGIE Caucus (ASC 2012)

1 Introduction

Sexuality and gender diversity rights in Southeast Asia are deeply controversial and vigorously contested. Debate and protest have been accompanied by both legislative reform and discriminatory violence. In some states, moral panics have been mobilised and the lives and well-being of sexuality and gender diverse people have come under threat. In others, changes in public policy and social norms have created new opportunities and freedoms, enabling people to live more open and fulfilling lives. There is no consistent pattern among states across the region and divergent trajectories appear to be developing. These dynamics are occurring at a time when the international human rights regime has explicitly incorporated a focus on the prevention of violence and discrimination in relation to sexuality and gender diversity. However, most Southeast Asian states do not recognise the need for such rights, and the regional block, the Association of Southeast Asian Nations (ASEAN), deliberately refrained from incorporating them in its own recently promulgated human rights regime.

By contrast, and partly in response, civil society organisations promoting an emancipatory politics of sexuality and gender diversity have proliferated. Many of these groups explicitly utilise rights politics as a platform for visibility, contestation and mobilisation. Their articulation of political struggle through a shared set of rights claims derives from common and shared experiences of violence and discrimination, and a visceral demand and hope for change. Rights claiming for people of diverse sexual orientation, gender identity expression and sex characteristics (SOGIESC) has become a potent mechanism for politicisation and participation and has been used to forge connections across the region and internationally.

Political participation using SOGIESC rights claiming in Southeast Asia has been extensive and diverse, encompassing a wide range of actors from the elite to the grassroots. The forms this political participation takes and the contexts in which it occurs are critical, leading to widely differential outcomes and contending dynamics. Some political and social elites maintain the 'ghost of Asian values', insisting that sexuality and gender rights are neocolonial impositions that have no local resonance (ASC 2018). 'The LGBTs' – where the acronym stands for people identified as lesbian, gay, bisexual and transgender (often augmented with I for intersex and Q for queer) – are here associated with Western identity and cultural categories argued to have no proper relation to the region. Many advocates and activists, however, see the merit and utility of such rights claiming, either on instrumental or substantive grounds, and argue for productive links between such new rights practices and the long histories of sexuality and gender diversity across the region (ASC 2018). In their rights advocacy, they utilise, often with qualification, varieties of both the SOGIESC and LGBTIQ nomenclature (a practice I will follow in this Element, as context dictates). Outcomes from such rights-based work have been significant and transformative: changes around gender recognition, anti-discrimination legislation, relationship regulation, media portrayal, access to health services and a range of other matters have been seen in some jurisdictions. In others, however, increased levels of state surveillance, discrimination, violence and persecution reinforce the impetus for further advocacy and protection.

Wherever SOGIESC rights claiming takes place, it occurs in an environment already riven by social and political conflict, power networks, material interests, ideological positioning and religious and ethnic contest. Struggles for authority and legitimacy produce ongoing dynamics of inclusion and exclusion. Rights claiming necessarily operates as a vector of politics, understood classically as the struggle over who gets what, where, when and how. And in that struggle, sexuality and gender are always already intersectional issues, imbricated with a wide range of other social conflicts (such as those involving class and ethnicity).

In this Element, the struggle for SOGIESC rights in Southeast Asia is understood within this broader context to show how making, engaging, contesting and constraining rights claims all feature as different forms of rights-related political participation. Neither rights claiming nor resistance to these claims can be properly understood without considering them as elements in a broader context of political (social and economic) activity. Without this perspective we cannot understand, for example, how Singapore can welcome gay tech workers while refusing to decriminalise homosexuality, or how a society with such a storied history of transgender ritualism as Indonesia can become embroiled in an LGBT moral panic. It is needed to understand why in Thailand, commonly understood as a queer haven, there are limitations on the social acceptance of gays and lesbians. Contextualising SOGIESC rights claiming in this way points us towards a more complex and sophisticated understanding of what is at stake when there is a conflict, a moral panic or a shift towards

SOGIESC inclusion in one or another policy arena; with it, we can look beyond immediate appearances to see the deeper structures that undergird SOGIESC conflicts. One objective of this work is to provide an introductory overview of that context, equipping readers to further develop a nuanced understanding of what is at stake in the region's disputes over sexuality and gender.

Beyond this, however, I want to make an argument about how we might interpret the development and spread of the use of rights claiming by sexuality and gender diverse communities in the region. I suggest that rights claiming in this way is a newly available mode of political participation, facilitated by regional and international developments, which connect local SOGIESC activity with rights-based movements on a range of different scales. These connections open new opportunities for political engagement on SOGIESC matters.

Modes of participation analysis examine who gets to participate in political decision-making, how they participate and with what consequences (Jayasuriya and Rodan 2007; Rodan and Baker 2020). 'Its essence', Gary Rodan argues, 'is to subject institutions of political participation in any regime to scrutiny over the nature and extent of contestation permitted or blocked through them' (Rodan 2018, 33; cf. Rodan 2022). A *mode of participation* itself is the amalgam of institutional structures and political ideologies that enable or constrain participation in political decision-making, its manner and justification (Jayasuriya and Rodan 2007, 774; Rodan and Baker 2020, 93). As Kelly Gerard emphasises, this amalgam shapes politics, making some forms of participation acceptable, and refusing others (Gerard 2014, 5). Both rights claiming in general and claiming SOGIESC rights in particular have become newly available as modes of political participation in Southeast Asia, precisely because of shifts in the amalgam of institutional structures and political ideologies.

Rights claiming, I suggest, can be understood as a distinctive mode of political participation. It is constituted with support from diverse ideologies which allow their normative commitments to be articulated as rights, and by a similarly diverse range of interlocking institutions (governmental and not) at different levels, which engage with rights discourse.

The formal ideological and institutional reference points come from the international human rights regime, under the auspices of the United Nations. This regime is a powerful tool for legitimating claims for political participation and representation. People appeal to it as they address social conflict at very local levels, as well as at larger scales. This points to the distinctive nature of rights claiming: it is fundamentally a normative act, which to function as a form of political participation requires support from a variety of institutional, social and ideological sources at different levels (local, domestic, regional, international) – even when these sources may be antipathetic to formal political, economic and social institutions.

Understood in this way, rights claiming differs in an instructive way from other modes of participation recently elaborated using this analysis. Rodan's work, for example, examines discrete mechanisms: nominated members of parliament, participatory budgeting and consultative representation in Singapore, the Philippines and Malaysia, respectively. Of modes in his range of cases, he observes: 'some are state based or state/trans-state sponsored while others are more autonomous from the state, with contrasting levels of inclusion in political participation through those sites; some entail individual participation while others admit collective organisation' (Rodan 2018, 33). This schema patterns Rodan's analyses, categorising these mechanisms using an individual/ collective and state/non-state matrix.

Rights claiming as a mode of participation is less amenable to being divided up in this way. While a given instance of rights claiming may emerge out of a site such as those Rodan examines, the act of rights claiming itself seeks to engender political participation across all dimensions of Rodan's schema: as a practice it depends on individual *and* collective participation, and is engaged with *and* against the state in an international context. This, I argue, is what makes rights claiming distinctive: the cross-cutting impact of its normative claim, and the need for institutional support across these dimensions for that claim to have purchase, to drive impact in contexts of social and political conflict. We can observe this too in the distinctive way in which its efficacy as a mode of participation cuts across different domains: rights are *moral* and *political* claims that require a combination of individual commitment, institutional support, legal infrastructure, economic provisioning and social legitimacy in order to gain purchase. Their full functioning requires a framework that connects the individual to the international, and civil society to intergovernmental organisation.

We can crystallise this second critical difference as one of *scale* (cf. Gerard 2014; Sinclair 2020). As a distinctive mode of participation, rights gain traction because the local site is connected to others: nationally, regionally and internationally. Indeed, the political ideology of human rights claims *universal* scale – a claim which is at once a key element of its success and a point of great ideological contention (Langlois 2001). The connections of rights politics travel through institutional structures that harness both individual and collective activity, and are based in both state and intergovernmental mechanisms and civil society. We may conceptualise these connections through the ideological reference point of the rights claim itself. The rights claim has potential traction as a mode of political participation for dealing with a local situation precisely because of the scale, at interlocking levels, of the diverse ideological and institutional networks that back it.

This leads us then to our specific purpose here: interpreting SOGIESC rights claiming in the region through this broader understanding of the rights claiming mode of participation. SOGIESC advocates present normative rights claims about sexuality and gender diversity through forms of rights-based political activity in contexts of social conflict across a series of interlinked scales: the local, domestic, regional and international. This Element is an introductory survey of how this political activity has been taken up by advocates and evolved as a mode of political participation.

SOGIESC rights claiming in the region emerges out of a range of historical and contemporary developments. Each nation has its own sexuality and gender diverse communities with complex and storied histories, which long predate the use of contemporary rights politics. I profile the context of SOGIESC rights claiming in five national cases: Indonesia, Malaysia, Singapore, the Philippines and Thailand. Critically, developments at this level are interlinked with regional and global shifts in SOGIESC rights institutionalisation and advocacy, especially through several contributing developments. One headline act was the establishment by a group of distinguished independent jurists, scholars and advocates of the Yogyakarta Principles (2007), which articulated SOGIESC protections already extant in international human rights law. In the same year, the United Nations established the new process of Universal Periodic Review (2007), which, as we shall see, became an important tool for SOGIESC advocates. Then, as noted, ASEAN instituted its own human rights regime (2009); controversially it excluded protection of sexuality and gender diversity, in turn precipitating a generative civil society response. The UN's Human Rights Council (HRC) also came out strongly in support of SOGIESC rights as human rights (early 2010s) and appointed an Independent Expert (IE) (2016) – with the inaugural occupant of this role being Vitit Muntarbhorn from Thailand. Activists, advocates, professionals and ordinary community members across civil society contributed to and engaged with these international developments, expanding the sites and scale of political engagement with SOGIESC rights claiming, and establishing it as an identifiable mode of political participation.

Rights, notwithstanding the qualifiers *human* or *universal*, are political instruments (cf. Chua 2022). They require a particular moral or normative imaginary, and specific institutions in order to gain traction on our material and social well-being. But these in turn always presuppose some or another political or ideological vision. The institutional and the ideological here are the two general components of modes of participation. Both can also be *played* politically, set to purposes that are tangential or even opposed to their ostensible normative ends. This too is part of the story of SOGIESC rights claiming: rights claims are not always engaged on their own terms, but can be incorporated within other, diverse, even seemingly contrary political agendas. A variety of critical and queer scholars have analysed such instrumentalisation in various contexts, including geopolitics, development assistance, aid, religious conflict and electoral politics (Bosia, McEvoy, and Rahman 2019; Duggan 2002; Gross 2018; Puar 2007; Rahman 2014; Rao 2020; Weiss and Bosia 2013 among others). SOGIESC rights claiming as a mode of political participation, as noted earlier, pays methodological attention to social conflict in context; it enables a critical analysis of the role rights play, for good and ill. It can contribute a sophisticated understanding of why and how rights come into the picture, what they are being used for and by whom, and what happens when specific rights are politicised and get drawn into social conflicts.

In the conventional story of how rights function, they require regimes, institutions and legal norms. In most critical respects, these elements are missing, incomplete or inchoate, when it comes to SOGIESC rights – and yet, the appeal to these rights persists and builds, constituting demands, claims and participation in the political space. Understanding the making of SOGIESC rights claims as a mode of participation suggests a way of theorising rights-based developments which addresses *how* they function in these contexts of social conflict, and which points to their value in generating political engagement, notwithstanding outcomes which, on conventional expectations of what rights should do, are poor. It transcends the limitations of analyses that might dismiss rights activity because of the weakness of formal institutions, the absence of legal systems or appropriate norms or because of (allegedly) mismatched cultural traditions. These dismissals tend to see rights claiming as a process that depends on the existence of legal and political institutions with a remit and the capacity to fulfil rights demands. In their absence, rights claiming is judged as just so much political theatre.

Seeing rights claiming *instead* as a tool with which to demand participation in a political process, by harnessing vectors of sociopolitical conflict, enables a more accurate reflection on how social movements utilise their claims (cf. Weiss 2017). An end point may eventually be fully adumbrated rights regimes, but none that do exist have emerged from anything other than an evolutionary and participatory political process. This points to one of the characteristic features of rights: that they are prefigurative and performative, calling themselves into existence by being claimed (cf. Zivi 2011).

Outline

Each of the sections of this Element focusses on a different constituent element of SOGIESC rights claiming understood as a mode of political participation: the region's own deeper history of sexuality and gender diversity; recent SOGIESC advocacy in five national cases; and regional advocacy, first with a focus on civil society and then through the lens of formal rights mechanisms. Each of these elements is of interest in their own right, but it is in their interaction together that we see the regional emergence of SOGIESC rights claiming as a mode of political participation, a concluding overview of which is offered in the final section.

A Regional History of Sexuality and Gender Diversity

Resistance to SOGIESC rights commonly situates them as alien imports: the influence of Western decadence or some form of neocolonialism. When this 'Asia versus the West' debate gains the headlines, it hides the long and varied history of sexuality and gender diversity within the region. While the articulation of this diversity through the rights claiming mode of participation is correctly understood as a newer phenomenon, the cultural histories and traditions of Southeast Asia are threaded through with diverse practices of sexuality and gender pluralism, practices with continuities into the present, where they proliferate and change, moulded by contemporary conditions. Remembering this diversity shifts the debate, demonstrating its political nature and the investment of power and interest in the manipulation of certain forms of social and ideological conflict through memory and forgetting. For advocates, the collective memory of indigenous and pre-colonial forms of life can play a significant role in contemporary cultural production and political participation.

Contemporary Cases

This section gives an overview of the recent trajectories of sexuality and gender politics in each of five national cases from the region: Indonesia, Malaysia, Singapore, the Philippines and Thailand. Across these cases, diverse and distinctive outcomes emerge as SOGIESC advocacy occurs within specific national contexts of social conflict and political participation. SOGIESC rights claiming can be observed at a range of sites and scales. It is layered into existing forms of sociopolitical conflict, shaping processes and outcomes. The differences between cases illustrate the complex and distinctive functioning of rights claiming as a mode of political participation. For example, rights claiming as a *legal method* is only available in some jurisdictions. Elsewhere, as a form of *political suasion* it operates in a different register, across a range of differently scaled sites (from local social groups to national political lobbying). Rights claiming also remains unavailable or unhelpful for some individuals and communities: rights politics is not a panacea, and SOGIESC rights claiming, here as elsewhere, will not meet the needs or be to the ideological taste of all.

Rights Advocacy

Changing focus from national narratives to rights organising, this section examines the ways in which sexuality and gender diverse people come together to support one another and engage in advocacy. The focus here is on the linkages between local, national and regional organising in pursuit of SOGIESC rights, through civil society organisation and in conjunction with formal rights regimes – thus emphasising the necessary element of scale in the rights claiming mode of political participation. The emergence of SOGIESC rights claiming benefitted from the inauguration of a regional human rights regime, with a critical and counter-intuitive element being the specific *omission* of SOGIESC rights from that regime. The creation of the regime nonetheless gave political legitimation to the use of previously suspect rights language, and enabled comparisons to best practice elsewhere – especially concerning the omitted rights. Together with National Human Rights Institutions (NHRIs), the UN's Universal Periodic Review process and – critically – a plethora of regional civil society organisations, an emerging architecture of human rights advocacy, can now be discerned across the region. SOGIESC civil society advocates have been prominent in all these developments.

SOGIESC Rights and Political Participation

In concluding this Element, I recapitulate my argument that SOGIESC rights claiming across Southeast Asia can be understood as a distinctive mode of political participation. Its signature extension across multiple sites and scales contributes a leverage and radical power for change that might not otherwise be possible, belying the often marginal status of its participants and supporting their desire to sustain an emancipatory and queer politics of sexuality and gender diversity in the region.

2 Historical Trajectories in Sexuality and Gender Pluralism

The histories and traditions of Southeast Asia are threaded through with diverse practises of sexuality and gender pluralism. A historical understanding of the region underscores that it is the rejection of this diversity which is new. Dédé

Oetomo made this point in a speech discussing the various regional traditions and their associated festivals. Oetomo, from Indonesia and a key figure in contemporary sexuality rights activism, noted a tendency to treat these traditions as 'decadent practices from the past'. He commented: 'I often say that in Southeast Asia, we do not adopt homosexuality from the West, but rather we adopt transphobia and homophobia from the West' (Oetomo 2013, 123). It was, after all, British colonialism that criminalised homosexual practice in several Southeast Asian polities, and Western impositions across social, cultural, economic and religious domains have consequentially reshaped perceptions of sexuality and gender in the region (Kirby 2013; Lennox and Waites 2013; Sanders 2009).

Southeast Asia's pre-colonial historical traditions and practices of sexuality and gender diversity are closely associated with ritual and religion. In some places, these practices persist in modified and contemporary forms. Transgender ritual specialists commonly held key symbolic roles in their communities. These included the *bissu*, spiritual leaders in Sulawesi, Indonesia; the *sida-sida*, priests in the service of the Sultans in Negeri Sembilan, Kelantan, Johor and elsewhere in Malaysia; *manang* who lived among the Iban people of Borneo and were held in high regard as dispute settlers; and the *warok* and *gemblakan* in Ponorogo, Indonesia, famed for their martial arts, who regularly performed at community events such as weddings (Petkovic 1999a, 1999b; Wilson 1999). Among the Ngaju Dayak people the transgender ritual specialists were known as the *basir*; in Burma they were the *nat kadaw*. In Thailand, Laos and Cambodia are the *kathoey*, often known today as 'ladyboys', a derogatory term that highlights the difficulty Southeast Asia's more fluid practices and conceptions pose to conventional Western notions of gender (Jackson 2001, 2011; Jackson and Sullivan 1999; Sanders 2020b). Continuing also into the present are a wide range of transgender communities, including the *waria* or *transpuan* (a more recently favoured term) in Indonesia; the *mak nyah, thirutambi* and *kua xing nan* in Malaysia; the *bakla, transpinoy* and *transpinay* in the Philippines; and the *apwint/apôn* or 'open/hider' in Myanmar (Al-Mohdhar and Ngu 2019; Coleman, Allen, and Ford 2018; Gilbert 2013; Graham Davies 2018; Khanis 2013; Rodriguez 2019, 372; Wijaya 2020, 161).

Positioning Southeast Asia as antipathetic to SOGIESC rights (notwithstanding the modern particularity of thinking about this diversity through rights) contrasts sharply with this storied history of complex, diverse and porous traditions. Anthropologist Michael Peletz takes this pluralism to be a key feature of the region, integral to understanding both the practices and traditions of sexuality and gender expression themselves, but also other aspects of its cultural formation over time. Peletz' account is a key corrective against the ideological centring of contemporary heteronormative forms.

Succinctly identifying pluralism as 'difference accorded legitimacy' (Peletz 2009, 7), Peletz theorises pluralism *from* the historical experience of the region, particularly regarding gender, sexuality and ethnicity. He offers the concept of 'gender pluralism' as a means for discussing the variations and vicissitudes of gender and sexual practices, as well as being a driver of broader forms of pluralism. 'It denotes', he says, 'pluralistic sensibilities and dispositions regarding bodily practices (adornment, attire, mannerisms) and embodied desires, as well as social roles, sexual relationships, and overall ways of being that bear on or are otherwise linked with local conceptions of femininity, masculinity, androgyny, hermaphroditism, and so on' (Peletz 2009, 11).

The early modern period, spanning the fifteenth and sixteenth centuries, is a period in which the common people experienced relative ease with respect to sexual and erotic practice and gender roles (Peletz 2009, 21). Travellers noted these characteristics:

> Portuguese observers of the sixteenth century reported that Malays were 'fond of music and given to love', the broader themes being that 'pre-marital sexual relations were regarded indulgently; … [that] virginity at marriage was not expected of either party'; that divorce was rather easily initiated by women and men alike; and that women were commonly included as heirs to rights over houses and land, in some cases being favored over male heirs. … Chinese and European observers emphasized similar patterns when writing about Javanese, Filipinos, Thais, Burmese, and other Southeast Asians.
> (Peletz 2009, 21, with internal quotes from Reid 1988, 153; cf. Peletz 1988, 1996; Wieringa 2000, 450–2)

More generally, and given his focus on the role of transgender ritual specialists in the early modern period, Peletz argues that 'in a wide variety of Asian cultural contexts, gender-transgressive behavior was both legitimate and sanctified and could bring considerable religious merit and prestige to its practitioners. … [R]eligiously informed cosmologies in the Asian region undergirded prestige hierarchies that valorized different forms and combinations of gender and sexuality and different ways of being human' (Peletz 2009, 36).

It is Southeast Asia's pluralism that is unique, with gender and sexuality the critical drivers of this uniqueness (cf. Ong and Peletz 1995). Unlike some regions where transgender and same-sex practices were 'bracketed exceptions' to otherwise prevailing heterosexual hegemonies, in Southeast Asia they were diffuse, contributing to a broader pluralistic ethos of embodied being in the world (Peletz 2009, 40, 81).

This pluralism, most clearly observed in the early modern period (1400–1500s), faced sustained erosion by transformations through the late modern period and into the present. The centralisation and increased canonicity of the region's religious traditions coincided with increased forms of hierarchy and legalism. These transformations left little room for the role of transgender ritual specialists, tended to close down space for same-sex sexualities and generally privileged the role of heterosexual males and undermined the centrality of women in ritual and public life. The decline in the status and well-being of women is of particular note: female literacy rates fell, poverty increased and exclusion from public office and economic and social autonomy became normative (Peletz 2009, 85).

A number of additional factors further drove these transformations, inter-linked through the advent and punishing impact of Western colonialism. The interactions with Western Christianity through missionary and state activity; the impact of commerce and capitalism; the territorial consolidation of states and their increasingly rationalised forms of rule; the ideologies of high modernity with their prejudices against the local, ritual and esoteric; developing scientific discourses on sex and evolution – all of these mitigated against the distinctive pluralism of the region (Peletz 2009, 85–86; cf. Reid 1988; Wieringa 2000).

The cumulative impact of these factors on the region's gender pluralism is decisive:

> When viewed from a long-term perspective, we see that many variants of transgendering and same-sex relations have been subject to processes of secularization and stigmatization, and that some of them have been heavily criminalized as well; and that most transgendered individuals have been redefined as contaminating rather than sacred mediators who are perversely muddling and enmiring the increasingly dichotomous terms of sex/gender systems long characterized by pluralism. Southeast Asia thus has much in common with other parts of the world that have been or are currently involved in transitions to (late) modernity, for generally speaking these transitions entail processes whereby once sacred mediating and liminal figures come to be redefined as contaminating, perverse, pathological, and categorically criminal if not explicitly treasonous. (Peletz 2009, 126–7)

There is a certain historical irony: that in the present time, the elite political, social and leadership classes of many states have sought to impose conservative, increasingly heteronormative codes for understanding sexuality and gender, against historical practices which they now represent as impure or decadent. The irony arises given that this was also the intention of Western imperial, colonial and orientalist forces, who until recently represented Southeast Asia 'as a limitless repository of deviance, extravagance, [and] eccentricity' urgently in need of the 'uplift' promised by agents of the Christian civilising mission (Peletz 2009, 5; cf. Wieringa 2000, 452).

The question of how the historical traditions of gender pluralism connect with the lives and practices of people today is a generative one for social movements in the region. Neither today's queer-phobic moral panics nor contemporary human rights advocacy can be understood as directly connected to these traditions, although both clearly emerge from the larger story of the impact and ongoing consequence of colonialism and Western modernity on the region. Rights advocacy is a key tool for those wanting to sustain communities and environments that allow contemporary forms of sexuality and gender pluralism to prosper and evolve, but rights discourse – a relative newcomer in the region (and indeed globally) – cannot, for precisely this reason, be an effective tool for connecting the past to the present, even as activists adopt it now for crucial advocacy work.

One response to how the past and present of sexuality and gender diversity can or should intersect has been through the use of art and culture. A recent region-wide example of this is the inaugural online Southeast Asia Queer Cultural Festival (SEAQCF), which premiered in February 2021 (ASC 2021c). Organised by the ASEAN SOGIE Caucus (ASC), the festival curated works that encompass literature, visual art, film, dance, music, poetry, memoire and activism, spanning the nations of the region. Driven by the connections between contemporary sexuality and gender diversity and historical predecessors and iterations, it employed memory, allusion, echoes of a lost collective past, retrieval and efforts to prevent erasure. The theme of 'Be/Longing' articulates a yearning desire for inclusion, care and respect, given that 'LGBTIQ people have always been part of the collective memories of the Southeast Asian community' (ASC 2021a).

This use of art and culture to reflect and refract historical and contemporary experiences of sexuality and gender diversity in the region is an avowedly political exercise, connecting to contemporary political participation. Accompanying the cultivation of a collective memory and building on the political purpose of the festival is its advocacy for an *alternative regionalism*:

> This refers to a collaborative process of holding accountable regional institutions (e.g. ASEAN) through people-oriented approaches within and outside State territories and functions. It involves strengthening the political leverage of transnational civil society and social movements to counter hegemonic regional governance arrangements that exclude marginalized groups. (ASC 2021a; cf. Aban and Sy 2020)

The invocation through art and culture of inclusive traditions of pluralism and diversity is an attempt to foster a different kind of discourse in the region – one which avoids the pitfalls and divisions of moral panic, but also one that sidesteps rights discourse, instead valorising a culture of pluralism and diversity through a re-telling of its own collective memory and tradition, on its own terms (rather than through the grammars of rights discourse) (Pang 2021). In this initiative, regional authorities are not the only target for critique and rebuke: the destruction and scars of Western colonialism, the consequences of criminalising laws and the savagery meted out by colonial agents against signs of queerness are all also part of the collective memory of the region, and feature prominently in the exhibits.

While the ensuing discussion will focus on contemporary debates about sexuality and gender diversity and the development of SOGIESC rights claiming, traditions and historical memory are refracted into the lives of the communities now using rights claiming to address discrimination and violence. The headline incidents of moral panic and human rights advocacy, law reform and political expediency are the stuff of day-to-day SOGIESC politics throughout the region. But they remain fundamentally structured by the enduring impact of colonialism, modernity, capitalism and geopolitics – as the specific recent histories of the five national cases to which we now turn attest.

3 National Case Studies

SOGIESC rights claiming as a mode of political participation operates at multiple scales: local, national, regional and international. Its emergence as a mode depends on the recent availability of rights claiming practices across these levels. National contexts play a key role in shaping rights claiming, as both its general practice and specific substantive claims – here, sexuality and gender – are connected to social contexts and conflicts in diverse and multifaceted ways. While people in both Singapore and Indonesia engage in SOGIESC rights claiming, for example, the shared ideological commitment at the heart of this mode of participation takes different institutional forms, is directed towards different immediate goals and is undertaken in diverse social, political, cultural and religious contexts. This is so, even while those same people are often involved in regional and even international forms of SOGIESC rights claiming, attempting to engage regional solidarity and activism across borders. This illustrates the scaled dimension of the mode, with the regional development of SOGIESC rights claiming (discussed in the next section) both building on the experience of national communities and engaging the broader emancipatory horizon that is part of the ideological makeup of rights claiming as a mode of participation.

In this section, we consider how recent developments have unfolded in each of five regional states: Indonesia, Malaysia, Singapore, the Philippines and Thailand. In these states, social movements, advocacy groups and individuals have used a range of strategies and methods in their attempts to shift the balance of social and political forces – often working across borders and boundaries, in solidarity and mutual aid. A wide variety of issues have generated attention, depending on the specific circumstances that provide the opportunity and need for active political engagement. Common to all is the effort to manage and frame SOGIESC matters in ways conducive to recognition as legitimate forms of political participation; equally common are struggle and conflict as forces and interests attempt to block such recognition. Outcomes vary widely, and among these cases a divergence appears to be developing between deteriorating environments in Malaysia and Indonesia, and more positive ones in Singapore, the Philippines and Thailand. Even when positive, however, outcomes remain insecure. This brief survey of national communities, then, illustrates how particular distributions of social power and conflict within specific (albeit interconnected) political environments shape the fight for SOGIESC rights.

Indonesia

Until very recently, Indonesia – the world's largest Muslim nation – had a broadly tolerant, if ambivalent, relationship with its sexuality and gender diverse populations (Wieringa 2019). As we have seen, its historical traditions involve transgender ritual specialists, and the continuing presence of communities such as the *bissu* of South Sulawesi have acknowledged cultural and social significance. *Waria* and *transpuan* communities can be found across the archipelago, along with people who identify themselves as gay, lesbian or bisexual, with LGBT being a commonly used collective acronym (although often in a distinctly pejorative and politicised manner, as we shall see). Nonetheless, Indonesian society in general is broadly traditional and conservative, maintaining an intensely heterosexual and familial domestic milieu (Platt, Davies, and Bennett 2018). Since 2016 in particular, the uneasy balance between this underlying heteronormativity and the ambivalent tolerance of sexuality and gender diversity has broken down. This was marked by the outbreak of an 'LGBT moral panic', and a steep escalation in the politicisation of a wide range of sexuality and gender-related issues. This development significantly alters the nature and trajectory of Indonesia's engagement with SOGIESC rights claiming as a mode of political participation, interrupting what appeared to be increased positive engagement, and forcing advocates into a more defensive position.

The extent of this change was unexpected, given that since the end of the New Order regime (1966–98), *Reformasi* and democratisation had set in play a wide range of social, cultural and political changes that transformed Indonesia. New spaces for queer organising had emerged, building on the gay activism that had taken place under the New Order, and furthering connections with the international LGBT movement. Civil society organisations dedicated to LGBT concerns had proliferated, as had engagement with human rights discourse and broader forms of advocacy (Khanis 2013).

Writing in the early 2000s, Baden Offord could comment that there was 'a thriving and dynamic gay presence in Indonesia' (Offord 2003, 108), a scene that could be easily observed in all the major urban centres, such as Jakarta, Yogyakarta, Surabaya and Denpasar. Indonesia was home to Southeast Asia's largest gay (primarily male-identified) organisation, GAYa NUSANTARA (established in 1987), with branches in over sixteen cities. 'What perhaps characterises Indonesian homosexuality in its relation to the wider polity', Offord says, 'is that it is not considered to be in contest at all' (Offord 2003, 104). Nonetheless, with societal norms constituted by the extended heterosexual family entrenched and backed in by the state and religion, individuals commonly found themselves subject to a range of double standards and hypocrisies around sexual practice. For gay men, this predominantly meant a life of seclusion within their families and communities. They were often married to women and had children, living lives of discretion and averse to confrontation – although these were lives that also practiced 'significant elasticity' with respect to their sexual identities (Offord 2003, 105).

By contrast, the lesbian community during the New Order had few activists and little visibility. At the organisational level it was largely silent and hidden (Khanis 2013). This was partly a consequence of the broader social expectation that women practice their sexuality only within heterosexual marriage (Wieringa 2000, 441), an expectation that made women's same-sex social forms even less visible because less legible to dominant social and identity understandings. As Blackwood's analysis suggests, the question of legibility is an issue within the lesbian community, too, extending from the local to the international. The *tombois*, *girlfriends*, lesbian men and masculine females of *lesbi* life throughout Indonesia were often obscured and hidden from one another, particularly outside of the major cities, because of the necessary secrecy of their lives; both this secrecy and the particular forms of their *lesbi* practice also obscured them from recognition by 'fully liberated global queers' observing from the outside (Blackwood 2010, 6–7, 2012).

By 2010, the New Order was firmly in the past, and Indonesia was consolidating as a democratic polity. In that year, however, conservative Islamic groups interrupted two major queer community gatherings, threating violence. The conference of the International Lesbian and Gay Association (ILGA) and the Q! Film Festival were both forcibly cancelled by vigilantes, while the state neglected to protect or support participants. Wijaya draws two conclusions from this turn of events:

> First, Indonesian LGBT activisms had become increasingly connected with transnational queer networks, enabling the activists to build cross-border coalitions, to expand their movements in the local landscape, and later, to openly assert rights claims for recognition and protection from the state. Second, the increased visibility of LGBT issues and movements in the democratic regime had been met with a rise in violent attacks, never witnessed during the authoritarian New Order rule. In addition to assaults from religious vigilantes, homosexuality and other non-normative sexualities were also increasingly codified and legally regulated, from the 2008 Pornography Law to some provincial ordinances; such practices were now explicitly marked as immoral behaviour, sexual deviancy, and even a criminal offence.
>
> (Wijaya 2020, 112–3)

The openness that democratisation and the end of the New Order had brought to the Indonesian polity, with its space for rights claims and connections at the global scale, had also allowed space for other forms of organising (cf. Hefner and Andaya 2018). Political mobilisation by religious conservative and fundamentalist forces proliferated, and the politicisation of anti-LGBT sentiment became increasingly widespread. In its wake, the count of violent and intimidatory incidents against sexuality and gender diverse individuals and communities began to mount (Boellstorff 2016; Wijaya 2020).

The Moral Panic

Suddenly, in 2016, the presence and increased visibility of the LGBT community registered with key governmental forces as a contest. State actors now depicted 'the LGBTs', a term they used in a disparaging manner, as a threat to concepts of Indonesian national identity and belonging. This threat required an answer, which in turn would reset the terms of public engagement on non-normative sexuality and gender matters. As Davies puts it, 'Sexual plurality might be tolerated but only as long as LGBT people remain collectively invisible and do not seek to become legitimate sexual citizens' (Graham Davies 2020). Group visibility and solidarity had become an affront, tapping into deep national fears as their opponents depicted LGBTs as a movement – a *gerakan.* Intan Paramaditha suggests that this term has deeply negative connotations drawn from the political history of communism within Indonesia. Drawing out these connections, Paramaditha observes that sexuality 'projects desire and fear in ways which illuminate how the nation is envisaged'. She continues:

> In the context of the nation, the phrase Gerakan LGBT (LGBT Movement) is often used to signify the national limit. Gerakan suggests transgression of a safe zone, a space when a harmless entity that we can 'tolerate' transforms into a national other. . . . The fear of Gerakan LGBT is precisely the fear of what is stipulated in Article 28 of the Constitution, 'the freedom to associate and to assemble'. It is the fear of publicness. (Paramaditha 2016)

Tom Boellstorff observes that 'the hundreds of pages of anti-LGBT statements' from early 2016 consistently repeat the claim that LGBT does not fit the national culture and should be rejected. This is a particularly poignant setback for community members, who seek to be *accepted* in the nation, and who view themselves as LGBT *Indonesians* (Boellstorff 2016).

The initial wave of this anti-LGBT national identity realignment manifested through a state-led moral panic about the 'LGBTs' – whose very existence propagandists framed as a '#DaruratLGBT', an 'LGBT Crisis' (Boellstorff 2016). The moral panic precipitated a radical change in Indonesian public discourse, with reference to matters of sexuality and gender spiking dramatically. 'LGBT' appeared in the mainstream Indonesian language press only a handful of times in 2013 and 2014, rising marginally in 2015, and then jumping to over 600 times in 2016. Wijaya comments, 'While LGBT was framed as "foreign" and "politically threatening," at the same time, it has also made "LGBT" a part of the everyday vernacular of many Indonesians' (Wijaya 2020, 3; cf. Ewing 2020; Listiorini 2020) – an important discursive prerequisite, even if negatively instantiated here, for SOGIESC rights claiming.

The seemingly small matter of the visibility of the LGBT community on a university campus triggered the moral panic. A brochure for an 'LGBT Peer Support Network' had been distributed at the University of Indonesia. Becoming aware of this, Minister for Research, Technology and Higher Education, Muhammad Nasir, stipulated that LGBT persons should be banned from university campuses. As Boellstorff comments, 'For a high-ranking government official to challenge a student brochure was unusual, but even stranger was that this same day the head of the People's Consultative Assembly, the highest legislative body in the nation, claimed in support of Nasir that "LGBT must be banned because it is does not fit with Indonesian culture"' (Boellstorff 2016).

Nasir walked his comments back following significant online and public reaction to his stance, but the nature of his retraction is instructive.

Acknowledging that he did not have the power to ban LGBT students from campuses and recognising the right of students to join organisations, he maintained, 'Our problem is when they are showing romance, kissing, and making love (in front of the public). . . . We are not against LGBTs but the activity' (Rappler 2016). The problem is in being seen, in being 'visible in solidarity', and by the way in which this social and political participation is received, as a challenge, contest or threat to national identity, culture and belonging (Graham Davies 2016).

The onslaught against such visibility was intense, unexpected and led from the top. Illustrative examples include the following: Defence Minister Ryamizard Ryacudu propounded a geopolitics of gay rights, portraying the movement as a form of modern warfare from the West designed to undermine Indonesia's sovereignty. A former minister, Tifatul Sembiring, incited violence on Twitter, calling on the public to kill any gay people they found. Vice-President Jusuf Kalla requested that the United Nations Development Program (UNDP) not fund community programmes that work against violence, discrimination and stigma for marginalised people. Agitation caused the temporary closing of Pondok Pesantren Waria al-Fatah in Java, the only Islamic school for transgender women. The Indonesian Psychiatric Association issued a statement identifying LGBT people as in need of psychiatric care, with homosexuality, bisexuality and transgenderism classified as treatable mental disorders. An Army general declared that LGBT people could not become soldiers. The Ministry of Youth and Sport barred LGBT youth from selection as Youth Ambassadors, requiring a certificate of 'normalcy' from participants' doctors. The government forced telecommunication and internet companies to remove LGBT content (such as gay emojis) and banned three gay dating apps (BBC News 2016; Boellstorff 2016; Wijaya 2020, 160). Anti-LGBT public protests were held; in Yogyakarta, protesters depicted homosexuality as an infectious virus and a disease (BBC News 2016).

In the midst of this anti-LGBT sentiment, rare voices of support were heard. One came from the president's close aid and Coordinating Minister for Legal, Political and Security Affairs Luhut Panjitan: 'We will protect LGBT individuals no matter who they are or what they do, because they are still citizens of Indonesia and have rights that should be protected' (Coconuts Jakarta 2016). Welcome as this was, the failure of the president himself to make an early statement significantly disappointed LGBT community members, who had supported his 2014 election campaign on the promise of a new era of tolerance in Indonesia (BBC News 2016). Later in the year, the president defended minorities, including LGBTs, against discrimination, requiring equality before the law and encouraging police protection where necessary – notwithstanding his view that LGBT people did not comport with Indonesian societal or religious norms (Wijaya 2020, 160). Rights protection, citizenship and indentitarian recognition are here layered into social conflict over norms regarding sexuality and gender.

Legal Challenges and Changes

The sudden, visceral rise of public anti-LGBT sentiment in 2016 consolidated within the Indonesian political landscape as an ongoing feature. It displaced any prospect of a new era of tolerance under President Jokowi, hoped for by queers and allies. By contrast, it facilitated an increasingly exclusionary environment, in line with established campaigns by conservative forces (such as the campaign against the 2011 Gender Equality Bill, *Rancangan Undang-Undang Kesetaraan Gender*, depicted as a pathway towards same-sex marriage; the bill subsequently stalled).

LGBTs had been pushed out of any safe zone they may have tentatively occupied into the transgressive space of the *national other*, subject to what Wijaya describes as 'a set of manoeuvres that produce new discursive technologies of surveillance, policing and control' from both state and non-state actors, collectively determining that there should be no future for LGBTs or queers under any description in Indonesia, and concurrently 'reorganiz[ing] Indonesian public understanding of bodies and sexualities . . .' (Wijaya 2020, 151, 152). The most striking manifestation of this 'reorganisation of public understandings' has been the attempt by conservatives to introduce a new legal regime for sexual conduct in Indonesia.

In 2016, a coalition, the Advocacy Team for a Civilized Indonesia (*Gerakan Indonesia Beradab*), headed by Rita Hendrawaty Soebagio, chair of the conservative Family Love Alliance (*Aliansi Cinta Keluarga*, AILA), submitted a legal challenge to Indonesia's Legal Code, through the national Constitutional Court, with the intent to make homosexuality and sex outside of marriage criminal offences (Wijaya 2020, 149–54). This set in train a series of legal and constitutional processes that carried on through the balance of the decade, providing a public locus for anti-LGBT sentiment, and a political focus for the relationship between sexuality and gender and Indonesian national identity (cf. Wieringa 2019).

In 2017, AILA first pursued this agenda by presenting a petition to Indonesia's Constitutional Court, with the purpose of making any form of extramarital sex illegal – a move intended to criminalise homosexuality, as well as police acceptable forms of heterosexuality (Wieringa 2019, 12). In their petition, AILA had argued that various articles in the Criminal Code 'threaten the resilience of families and therefore of Indonesia itself' (Reuters 2017). The Court voted against the petition 5/4, on the basis that existing laws did not conflict with the Constitution; the Court did suggest, however, that the plaintiff could take the matter up with Parliament, which was then deliberating on reform to the Criminal Code – an implied tacit endorsement of the cause (Davies 2020).

Drafts of the revisions of the Criminal Code from the parliamentary commission became public in early 2018, and included regulation of extramarital sex, same-sex relations and cohabitation, all previously unregulated. These proposed changes were understood to be widely supported within the parliament, as well as by a broadly conservative electorate (Reuters 2018). However, they also precipitated significant opposition, including concerns about 'overcriminalisation' from major political parties, the likelihood of a Constitutional Court challenge and international criticism (Llewellyn 2018). When debate in the House of Representatives commenced on the bill, Speaker Bambang Soesatyo emphasised that the legislation would curb 'homosexual excesses' (Deutsche Welle 2018). As the public became aware of the extent of the proposed changes – including implications for freedom of speech, discrimination, reproductive rights, privacy law, blasphemy and the recognition of 'living law' (which could include discriminatory customary laws and Islamic by-laws) – there were mass demonstrations and violent clashes as protesters sought to meet with the House Speaker. President Joko Widodo finally intervened, and the legislation was held over, although it remained on the National Legislation Programme for the 2020–2024 session (The Jakarta Post 2020). Parliament is also considering the so-called Family Resilience Bill, introduced in 2020 by AILA-linked conservative forces, pursuing the objectives of their earlier petition. The bill explicitly intends to entrench a conservative heteronormative vision of the traditional family; among its targets are LGBTs: marked as deviant, they are recommended for rehabilitation treatment in government-run institutions (Bexley and Bessell 2020; VOI 2020).

Thus, Indonesia's relationship with its sexuality and gender diverse population remains ambivalent, if now with an increased sense of political threat, a greater incidence of both societal violence and police brutality and significantly reduced opportunity for visible political participation. SOGIESC rights protection and advocacy increasingly go unnamed, under the flag of rights for marginalised or minority groups. Rights claiming as a general mode of political participation remains, and, as we will see in the next section, expands with Indonesia's role in the new ASEAN rights regime. This provides critical support and continued avenues for advocates to incorporate SOGIESC concerns. However, discretion is increasingly important for the maintenance of safety and belonging, as the culture's famous tolerance for diversity develops a noticeably foreshortened horizon on matters of sexuality and gender.

Malaysia

Governed by a dominant-party electoral authoritarian regime since its independence in 1957, Malaysia was launched into unfamiliar political territory as counting came to a close in 2018's fourteenth general election, GE14 (Weiss and Hazis 2020). The ruling coalition, the Barisan Nasional (BN, National Front), was ousted by a new coalition, Pakatan Harapan (PH or Pakatan), the Alliance of Hope: the hope being for a 'new' Malaysia, in which the corruption infecting the class of elite politicians could be addressed, and accountability embraced.

Some in Malaysia's LGBTIQ community also understood Pakatan's win to offer tacit hope for increased political participation, through the promise 'to build an inclusive and moderate' nation (Nufael 2018). The coalition had vowed to pursue universal human rights as one of its key priorities, a promise that advocates took to include the human rights of LGBTIQ people, to this point a criminalised and marginalised population (Cho 2019). An increased level of support for SOGIESC rights claiming seemed possible.

The coalition's candidate for prime minister, were they to win, was Mahathir Mohamad, former strongman and long-serving BN prime minister (1981–2003). His earlier rule was synonymous with a refusal of human rights, especially for homosexuals (Langlois 2001) – hardly an auspicious start. In the event, the Pakatan government proved politically unstable and short-lived. It fell in February 2020, replaced by another coalition, the Perikatan Nasional (PN), under the new prime minister Muhyiddin Yassin. Muhyiddin, though, was also unable to contain the political instability, and the prime ministership passed on in August 2021 to his deputy, Ismail Sabri Yaakob, the vice president of the United Malays National Organisation (UMNO) – the driving party of the pre-Pakatan BN government.

This ongoing political realignment further diminished hopes of democratic consolidation and confirmed premonitions of a stalling human rights agenda. The associated political dynamics exacerbated the climate of fear and insecurity Malaysia's LGBTIQ community experienced. While the upset at the ballot box in 2018 has not translated into rights advances or democratic consolidation, the rupture raised expectations about participation and inclusion; instead, all that has been seen is a further cycle of elite political fragmentation. With it, any hope for increased formal embrace of human rights in general, and of SOGIESC rights in particular, has been discarded. To track the impact of these developments, we first review the situation before GE14, then detail the Pakatan transition and its fallout.

Before the Transition

Homosexuality is formally illegal in Malaysia. At independence, the new state inherited the infamous British colonial law known as Section 377 – although this code (part of the 1936 Straits Settlement Penal Code, also adopted by Singapore) was not uniformly employed across all Malaysia's thirteen states until 1976. In 1989 it was significantly amended, to clearly criminalise anal and oral sex for all persons, gay or straight (Radics 2021). In addition to the federally mandated Criminal Code, each state also implements its own Shariah laws, which apply sanctions to Muslim residents and citizens in matters related to family and religion. These laws prohibit homosexuality and criminalise non-normative gender expression, the 'posing as someone of a different sex', producing an ever-present risk of incarceration (and concomitant police violence) for trans people (HRW 2014).

The criminalisation and repression of homosexuality was an important element of the discourse of Asian values, which Mahathir championed during his earlier premiership (1981–2003), particularly during the 1990s, extending institutionalisations of heterosexuality and homophobia which had modernised and purified the diversity of earlier local and regional transgender and same-sex practices. In Mahathir's values discourse, homosexuality and human rights were both Western practices, which Malaysians should not hesitate to reject. They were instead to embrace strong and stable (not to say authoritarian) government, a religious public culture connected to a conservative interpretation of the Islam of the Malay majority, responsibilities rather than rights and traditional moralities (read as forms of pious heteronormative familialism). Mahathir contrasted these norms at every available opportunity with the hedonism, individualism, materialism and sensual gratification that he articulated as the very definition of the West. He posited Asia and the West as monolithic and opposed in their value orientations – a setup that itself deployed a 'reverse orientalism ', or occidentalism, in order to make the case (Langlois 2001; Lawson 1999).

The consequences of Mahathir's deployment of Asian values for Malaysia's sexuality and gender diverse populations were significant and continue to the present. People and communities still connected to traditional forms of regional transgenderism and same-sex practice were marginalised, with increased intensity from the mid-1990s (Peletz 2009, 204), a time marked by both the modernising New Economic Policy and its successors (1971–), designed to create new urban Malays, and the Asian Financial Crisis of 1997–1998. While government policy pushed actively for urbanisation, seeking to attract populations to the big cities, Malaysian political discourse used Asian values as a brake against the development of cosmopolitan cultures, such as those one might see in nearby Bangkok. The government banned 'transvestites and gays' from radio and TV in 1994, with the health minister declaring: 'We do not want to encourage any form of homosexuality in our society' (Peletz 2009, 205). A crackdown on gay clubs followed. Gay events were cancelled by government edict. Malay-Muslim participants in *mak nyah* beauty contests were arrested. Prosecutions involving transgendered people were sensationalised, both by the media and also by the government, with the latter insisting that 'gender woes' were at risk of plaguing *all* families. A government minister declared: 'Parents need to be told the importance of bringing up their children according to the child's natural gender', and the administration tasked state religious and social welfare bureaus to ensure correct parenting, to establish a zero tolerance environment designed to prevent 'the problem of transvestites' (Peletz 2009, 210). A strategy and trajectory had been set whereby sexuality and gender minorities were simultaneously marginalised and sensationalised in order to implement a conservative social ideology, itself designed to variously slow, distract from and mask the rapid social changes economic policy was driving.

The instrumentalisation of non-normative sexuality played out most dramatically on the national stage, in the realm of elite politics. In September 1998, Mahathir's Deputy and Finance Minister, Anwar Ibrahim, was charged, among other alleged offences, with five counts of sodomy. These charges are almost universally understood to have been politically motivated by Mahathir to prolong his own political supremacy in the face of his popular deputy and rival. In 2004, after a long legal process, the Federal Court overturned Anwar's sodomy conviction. However, in 2008 fresh allegations were made – again, according to Anwar, on political grounds. A further complex and lengthy legal process and years of imprisonment then followed. He eventually received a full pardon from the king in 2018.

The impact of the charges against Anwar on Malaysian politics and society generally cannot be overstated: it precipitated a range of political realignments and new social imaginaries. The immediate consequences for LGBTQ people involved further repression, marginalisation, discrimination and violence. Political leaders used the accompanying media frenzy with great effect to extend and disseminate sentiment against all forms of non-normative sexuality and gender expression. Police raids against clubs and a wide range of other locales increased in frequency and intensity, with concomitant consequences: arrests, detention, drug testing and publicity. Community-based vigilante groups, intent on eliminating any form of same-sex sexuality in Malaysia, reinforced the police. Supporting these groups, in turn, was a network of often covert organisations, with close government links. The silver lining in an otherwise very dark cloud was that this public naming of homosexuality in Malaysia was an acknowledgement of its presence; within the fear of its contagion could be discerned a certain denaturalising of the claims otherwise found in Mahathir's Asian values discourse about sexuality and gender (tan beng hui in Peletz 2009, 224).

The Anwar affair still shadows national politics and the politics of sexuality in Malaysia. Anwar received his full pardon in 2018 in part so that he could be lined up – twenty years late – to take over the prime ministership from Mahathir once the latter had settled the new PH coalition government into place. Right on cue, further allegations of sodomy emerged, this time from within Anwar's own People's Justice Party, on the eve of its annual conference in 2019 (tan and Queer Lapis 2020; Kumar 2019). Earlier that year, gay sex videos appeared purportedly of Anwar's main rival in the party, Azmin Ali; he, too, claimed intra-party sabotage (with speculation including Anwar's involvement), confirming the utility of such claims to wreak political havoc. On this occasion, however, it was not sodomy accusations that denied Anwar the premiership, but the collapse of the political coalition of which his party was a member.

Qualified Optimism for a New Malaysia?

Pakatan campaigned on a human rights and anti-corruption platform. On many of its big-ticket items, it failed to deliver. It did not repeal the Sedition Act, nor end the death penalty; it did not ratify UN human rights treaties; it took U-turns on signing the Rome Statute of the ICC and the UN treaty on racial discrimination (Santiago 2019). For the LGBT community, disappointment with Pakatan registered immediately and was felt viscerally, as the coalition failed to protect community members from violence and discrimination. A sequence of disturbing events unfolded soon after Pakatan came to power. They started with the outing of a government aide in the office of the Minister for Youth and Sports, Numan Afifi, as not only a gay man but also a gay rights activist. Unsustainable levels of harassment from those who thought such values unsuitable in a government official led to his resignation. The Minister of Religious Affairs then disparaged the 'LGBT lifestyle' in Parliament and re-affirmed the government's intention to 'reach out' to the LBGT community with seminars, camps and campaigns – code for a continuation of gay conversion programmes. The minister also authorised the removal of portraits of two prominent LGBT activists from an arts exhibition in Penang, on the basis that the promotion of LGBT culture was against the government's position. Two women in Parti Islam Se-Malaysia (Pan-Malaysian Islamic Party, PAS)-led Terengganu were convicted (under state-level Shariah law) of attempting to have lesbian sex in a car, for which they were fined and publicly caned – an unprecedented punishment.

These and a range of other incidents were arrayed together in a document the activist organisation Pelangi Campaign distributed under the title '100 days Malaysia Baharu: LGBTQ people continue to be hunted down post 14th General Election' (tan 2019, 2; Pelangi Campaign 2018). tan beng hui comments, 'Saddened, disappointed and angered, those critical of the new regime's actions maintained that intolerance, hatred and violence were not part of the Malaysia they had voted for nor envisaged under the PH government .... . Overall, the loudest protests were about how continued "state-sponsored homophobia and transphobia" had accentuated discrimination against LGBTs during what many PH supporters had assumed would be a time of transition to a more progressive, tolerant and egalitarian society' (tan 2019, 2).

In her analysis of events during the first 100 days of the new administration (optimistically dubbed 'Malaysia Baharu', or New Malaysia), tan beng hui suggests that while Pakatan's response was disappointing and even dispiriting for the LGBT community, there was some evidence that Pakatan politicians were attempting to shift the terms of the official response to the 'LGBT question'. Mahathir said he was concerned that institutions like Jakim (*Jabatan Kemajuan Islam Malaysia* – Department for Islamic Development) were promoting a version of Islam that was 'cruel, harsh and unreasonable'. Here Mahathir was taking on the religious establishment and, hence, the ethnic Malay majority, playing a high-stakes game for reform – one that he appeared to lose when Pakatan fell to Perikatan Nasional in early 2020. tan beng hui suggests that Mahathir's shift of emphasis could be discerned in the government's responses to the incidents noted from the first 100 days, and to the LGBT question more broadly. On the Terengganu caning incident, for example, not only did the Cabinet make an unprecedented public statement on the matter, but it did so in terms that rebuked the state level Shariah Court for an unjust outcome that failed to show compassion. Similarly, Deputy Prime Minister Wan Azizah Wan Ismail's comment that 'LGBTs have the right to practise whatever [it is] they do in private' could not have been made under the previous regime; comments that Deputy Women's Minister Hannah Yeoh made against hate speech and violence after brutal public assaults on trans women were also unprecedented (tan 2019, 10–11). Collectively these nuances hinted at the possibility of a different approach to SOGIESC rights claiming.

A 'Newer' Malaysia: Back to the Future

Unable to contain political infighting over Mahathir-succession politics, and in the face of concerted undermining by their political opponents, the Pakatan Harapan coalition fell apart in February 2020. In its place followed (at the time of writing) two different coalition governments and prime ministerships, each looking more like the pre-2018 BN coalition than its predecessor, but each also weakened by the political infighting, and both helped and hindered in their bid for power by the COVID-19 pandemic.

The consequences for Malaysia's queer community have not been positive. LGBT people have become an open target for forces needing to establish their Islamist or Malay nationalist bona fides (FMT 2021). One key episode saw the then religious affairs minister, Zulkifli Mohamad, issue a call for trans people to be arrested and educated back to 'the right path', both confirming the government's normative position (Sukumaran 2020) and generating condemnation by groups such as the International Commission of Jurists (Tee 2020). The trope itself has a long and well-understood use, accompanied by an equally long history of criticism for the state-sanctioned and funded 'rehabilitation' practices it denotes (Queer Lapis 2020). In addition to such outbursts, there have been moves to consider increasing LGBT criminal penalties under the Shariah Courts (Criminal Jurisdiction) Act, a move the Malaysian Bar and SUHAKAM, the NHRI, oppose. Civil society group Justice for Sisters has argued that the move is unconstitutional (JFS 2021), while opposition parties argue that the government should focus on the COVID-19 pandemic, rather than vilifying queers (HRW 2021).

While subsequent political ructions make it unclear whether such moves will proceed, they surely indicate that the hope for an expansion of civil liberties and religious freedom Pakatan Harapan's 2018 electoral upset fostered is firmly in abeyance, following the coalition's loss of power. Nonetheless, events have given the discourse of rights claiming significant prominence, which has extended to SOGIESC rights to some measure, despite the failure of political reform. While this limits political participation to oppositional and advocacy spaces domestically, as we will see in the next section, this activity connects with rights claiming at regional and international levels. Locally, the multiplication of instabilities in Malaysian politics – from the end of a sixty-year run in government to a pandemic-induced emergency with a rotating prime ministership – makes it hard to gauge where interests lie and how the lines of power will reassemble. The prevailing shift in power back to some form of pre-Pakatan coalition, however, does not bode well for progressive reforms in Malaysian politics, least of all for queers.

Philippines

Quezon City, in Metro Manila, was the site of the first gay pride march in Asia, in 1994, held in the wake of the people-power movement that toppled the Marcos dictatorship. In another first, the 2000s saw candidates from Ladlad, a political party set up by the Philippines gay community, the only party of its type in the world, contest in national elections (Sintos Coloma 2013; Soriano 2014). More recently, 2016 saw an open trans woman, Geraldine Batista Roman, elected to Congress. Homosexuality is *not* criminalised in the Philippines, and while legal protections against violence and discrimination remain deeply insecure and contested, there exists robust and engaged LGBTQ community organisation in political, legal, cultural and business circles. People have relative freedom to express non-heterosexual identities, to organise and associate, and to be recognised in society. These conditions facilitate political participation on SOGIESC issues, with rights claiming and law reform significant domains for engagement at local and domestic levels, and the Philippines providing an important base for regional organising (see discussion of ASC in the next section).

While this environment contributes to the Philippines having a reputation as one of the most friendly and accepting societies for LGBTIQ people in the region, Filipino queers experience a distinctly 'contradictory' reality (Cardozo 2014, 6). Critically, while 'a degree of passive tolerance towards the LGBT community exists in the Philippines, this tolerance and leniency do(es) not equate to equal protection by the law' (Soriano 2014, 24). Surveys suggest that a significant majority of Filipinos think homosexuality should be socially acceptable (63 per cent for those over fifty years of age, 73 per cent for those thirty to forty-nine and 80 per cent for those aged eighteen to twenty-nine (Poushter and Kent 2020)). At the same time, dominant religious and associated sociocultural institutions and authorities are viscerally opposed to any normalisation of non-heterosexual forms of sexual practice or gender identity. The influence of the Catholic church, in particular, with its family-centred traditional morality, extends throughout all facets of culture and society. Nearly 80 per cent of the population adhere to the religion, and while some religious communities are known to extend compassion and even a welcome environment to LGBT people (Shine 2019), this is generally heavily caveated: queer people seeking religious community are commonly expected to be celibate or to undergo 'conversion therapy' – a practice that is medically discredited and that the UN has condemned (UN HRC and SOGI Independent Expert 2020). The Catholic church remains formally opposed to homosexuality and contributes a doctrinaire heteronormativity to society, politics and culture. This in turn fuels prejudice, discrimination and intolerance (Gamboa et al. 2020, 4–5).

The archipelago itself has long historical traditions of sexuality and gender diversity which predate the arrival of Catholicism. However, in the two major periods of colonialism the Philippines experienced, norms gained purchase that denied the legitimacy of non-heteronormative sexual practice and gender identities. The first period, under Roman Catholic Spain, 'introduced a powerful sexual ideology of *machismo* that [. . .] formed the foundation for misogyny and homophobia'. When Spain ceded the territory to the United States, secularism became the formal norm. However, 'rather than diluting religious homophobia, the Americans' biomedical models (mainly drawing from Freudian psychiatry) merely tagged homosexuality with a new label – that of "sickness" – [added] to the old one of "sin"' (Tan 1995).

The contemporary LGBTIQ community then, while not criminalised like elsewhere in the region, inherits an environment structured by heteronormative notions of masculinity, femininity and familialism sanctioned by powerful religious doctrine and medicalised references. Political leadership at the national level is divided: strongman President Duterte's support for SOGIESC rights is erratic and inconsistent, and while pro-LGBTQ members of Congress are stalwart and effective, they have thus far failed to prevail over conservative opponents to win critical votes. Few legal protections exist when people find themselves faced with discrimination, violence, exclusion and marginalisation, whether in the home, the workplace or health and educational institutions or from police, military and security services (ASC 2017). SOGIESC issues remain widely socially stigmatised, with harsh material and social consequences (ASC 2017). In particular, violence against trans people has taken on a particularly high public profile, with the cases of Jennifer Laude (murdered by a US soldier in 2014) and Gretchen Diez (arrested while trying to use a women's restroom in Quezon City in 2019) provoking significant political and social mobilisation.

SOGIE Equality Bill Debate

At the commencement of the Eighteenth Congress of the Philippines in February 2020, a bill was filed, titled, 'An Act Prohibiting Discrimination on the Basis of Sexual Orientation and Gender Identity and Expression (Sogie) and Providing Penalties Therefor'. Its sponsors were Kaka Bag-ao, Geraldine Roman and Tom Villarin in the House of Representatives, and Risa Hontiveros in the Senate. The bill's explanatory note articulates clearly the need for specific anti-discrimination protections for LGBTQ people. Notwithstanding constitutional guarantees of human rights and equality before the law for all men and women, the bill argues:

> Prejudicial practices and policies – mostly unstated and unwritten – based on sexual orientation and gender identity severely limit the exercise and enjoyment of the basic rights and fundamental freedoms in schools, workplaces, commercial establishments, the civil service, even the security services. LGBT students are denied admission or expelled from schools due to their sexual orientation or gender identity. Companies block the promotion and stymie the career advancement of gay or lesbian employees due to the deeply embedded notion that homosexuality denotes weakness. Laws such as the current anti-vagrancy law are also abused by the law enforcement agencies to harass gay men. It is therefore imperative to define and penalize practices that discriminate against LGBTs.

The bill, the latest iteration in a series of such bills, has become a cause célèbre in Filipino politics. Senator Miriam Defensor-Santiago and Representative Etta Rosales filed the initial version in the Eleventh Congress in 2000. In the Twelfth Congress, the House of Representatives approved a version, but it failed in the Senate. Subsequent iterations failed to pass in either chamber.

The Seventeenth Congress saw a breakthrough in the progress of the bill: in 2017, it passed the House of Representatives with a final vote of 198 to 0. The bill could now once again be considered by the Senate. This time around, in addition to the left-wing Akbayan Citizens' Action Party, including Senator Risa Hontiveros, the bill's sponsor, trans woman Senator Geraldine Roman also promoted the bill, galvanising a concerted effort to advance the now two-decades-long campaign. This effort, however, entrenched opposition from establishment and religious forces. In mid-2018, the Senate elected a new leader, opposed to the bill, who then deployed delaying tactics to prevent deliberation and voting. Through 2018 and into 2019, public debate ran hot. Cases of discrimination and violence against LGBT people came to light and generated public protest (Calera 2019; Morgan 2019). Opposition was stirred by false claims that the bill authorised same-sex marriage, and that the values it promoted were 'imported' and disregarded Filipino culture (Vergara 2019). In the end, opponents ran down the clock, and the bill was automatically archived as the Seventeenth Congress reached the end of its term.

As the SOGIE Equality Act returned to be considered again in 2020, this time by the Eighteenth Congress, the political debate once again shifted. Opposition forces doubled down, with escalated rhetoric from the religious establishment reflecting US-style culture war tactics. Events taking place within the queer community, meanwhile, highlighted the need for the Act. LGBT protesters found themselves targeted and detained at a Pride event protesting government anti-terrorism legislation, itself widely condemned as a threat to the rule of law (Beltran 2020; Thoreson 2020b). Shaming and humiliation of LGBT people emerged in a local incident that was publicised live on social media, under the guise of public health law enforcement for COVID-19 (Thoreson 2020a). The military released a position paper opposed to the SOGIE Equality Act (Panti 2020). And President Duterte's high-profile decision to pardon a US Marine convicted for killing trans woman Jenifer Laude in 2014 sparked outrage and urgent calls for the Act to be passed (Nonato 2020; Palo 2020).

While the fate of the bill in the Eighteenth Congress is unknown at the time of writing, supporters worry that it will be sidelined by alternative proposed legislation, a strategy that President Duterte appears to support. The House of Representatives, now dominated by a bloc allied with the president and prepared to channel his populist patriarchal machismo, is likely to favour that bill, which would mandate 'equality for all', rather than (as erroneously claimed) 'special rights' for LGBT people (Beltran 2020; Mendez 2019). Such a bill would be modelled after one that Duterte passed earlier in his career, when mayor of Davao. The dangers of such an approach are clear, however: that it would fail to specify discrimination based on sexual orientation or gender identity and expression, and that it would fail to provide the necessary executable penalties for specific common forms of discrimination, as detailed in the current SOGIE Equality Act. There is no unified position in the queer community as to whether it is better to support a SOGIE-specific act or settle for a more universal anti-discrimination law.

While progress on legislative measures to protect against discrimination and violence on the basis of SOGIE has been consistently forestalled at the *national* level, some *local* governments within the Philippines have made more headway. Quezon City addressed the question of employment-related discrimination for homosexuals, in both the public and the private sectors, with a local ordinance in 2003; in 2014 it also instituted a 'gender fair' ordinance, which adds broader SOGIE protections, as well as provisions for equal pay and sensitivity training (Rappler 2019). Since Quezon City's initial ordinance, more than twenty-five other local government units have put in place either general anti-discrimination ordinances or ordinances that specifically address sexual orientation or gender identity (Chase 2017; Jocson and Adihartono 2020). In the absence of progress at the national level, activists have favoured local jurisdictions in which change can be achieved, notwithstanding some variability around meaningful consultation with community groups and in follow-through. Generally, LGBT people and organisations have limited access to and are underrepresented in law-making institutions in the Philippines, including on issues that affect them directly – notably, in the health domain, including HIV/AIDS (UNDP and USAID 2014).

Relationship Recognition

While the principal focus of political debate has been on the SOGIE Equality Act, there have also been attempts to address the question of relationship recognition. The Philippines Family Code of 1987 explicitly indicates that marriage is between a man and a woman. This requirement was not articulated in the 1949 Code it replaced, nor is it in the Constitution. In 2015, a young, openly gay lawyer, Jesus Nicardo Falcis III, sought to have the same-sex marriage prohibition in the Family Code overturned on the basis that it was unconstitutional. In a petition filed with the Supreme Court, he argued that allowing only heterosexuals to enter into civil marriages violates other Filipinos' constitutional rights, including to equal treatment and 'marital autonomy' (Bernal 2015). Both the petition and its argument were unprecedented in the Philippines, and the novelty intrigued the Supreme Court sufficiently for it to accept the petition and sit for oral arguments in 2018 (Fonbuena 2018). In its 2019 ruling, the Court denied Falcis' plea, primarily on technical grounds; in 2020, it closed off the possibility of judicial reconsideration. In rejecting the petition, however, the Court did recognise the long history of marginalisation and discrimination against LGBTIQ people and advised that any change in the current Family Code was a matter that should be pursued through the Congress (ABS-CBN News 2020; The Jakarta Post 2019). Indeed, the text of the Court's decision shows it to fall within what Geronimo describes as 'an emerging line of jurisprudence … that more favorably considers the plight of LGBTQI+ individuals and is more receptive to SOGIESC equality' (Geronimo 2020; cf. *Falcis* v. *Civil Registrar General, G.R. No. 217910* 2019).

During the period in which the Court considered Falcis' petition, Congress was, in fact, attempting to address the question via the legislative route. A bill to effect changes to the Family Code of the Philippines was filed in 2017, with support from the Speaker of the House; however, it failed. The bill was re-filed in the current Congress in 2019 yet faces concerted opposition and has little hope of progressing to, let alone through, the Senate. An earlier bill from 2011 would at least have recognised same-sex marriages established outside the Philippines had it gained support (Herrera 2020).

As with the SOGIE Equality Bill, the Catholic church is a powerful force in this debate, and it has utilised the full extent of its influence to prevent relationship recognition. While some church leaders support anti-discrimination legislation on the basis of the equal moral worth of all persons, despite their doctrinal discomfort with LGBTQ identities and practices, support for civil unions or marriage is rare from religious leaders and is firmly against Catholic doctrine. As a joint submission of LGBTIQ-focused civil society organisations for the Philippines' 2017 UPR review notes:

> The Catholic Bishops Conference of the Philippines issued a statement in August 2015 urging all Catholic believe[r]s to 'resist all attempts to normalize homosexual behavior and homosexual unions in their culture' and to 'oppose all gravely unjust laws that contravene both divine law and natural law – including all laws that legalize homosexual unions'. The said statement while preaching mercy and understanding towards LGBTIQ people continues to consider homosexuality as a 'familial shame'. (ASC 2017, 4)

Among the general population, attitudes are harder to divine. The House of Representatives ran a poll on the issue in 2019, which had respondents running at 48 per cent for and 51 per cent against same-sex marriage (ABS-CBN News 2019); the poll was taken down after receiving criticisms, including from the Lesbian and Gay Legislative Advocacy Network (LAGABLAB) (Coconuts Manila 2019). The results of the House poll are notably different from a separate poll, a year earlier, which indicated only 22 per cent support for same-sex marriage (Talabong 2018).

The president is currently understood to support civil unions, but not marriage, for same-sex partners (ABS-CBN News 2019), although he had previously asserted: 'I am for (same-)sex marriage if that is the trend of the modern times. If that will add to your happiness, I am for it' (Tubeza 2017). However, as one commentator put it, Duterte's 'view on the matter appears to shift depending upon how he feels about the Catholic Bishops' Conference of the Philippines on any given day' (Cook 2019). As with his inconsistent comments on the SOGIE Equality Act, the president's contributions to the debate can generate more confusion than clarity (cf. Mendez 2019). Generating further confusion, Duterte's camp has attempted to leverage electoral appeal through a new vehicle, LGBT Pilipinas (not to be confused with Ladlad, which also competes under the party list system) – a move that received significant pushback from the LGBT movement at large. A statement signed by more than forty organisations asserted: 'President Duterte's track record of providing only bogus support for the LGBTQIA+ community demonstrates that he is no ally to us' (Villaruel 2021).

While the Philippines remains one of the 'friendlier' places to be queer in the region, little is guaranteed with respect to safety, security, health, discrimination or political recognition. The relative freedom for engagement with SOGIESC issues has enabled rights claiming as a mode of political participation not just in advocacy and civil society spaces, but also through the mechanisms of formal politics, and at all scales: local, national and (as we shall see later in this Element) international – even if systemic changes have been few. The imbrication of sexuality and gender issues with other societal conflicts is a key element that makes it difficult to achieve secure rights-based outcomes.

Singapore

Singapore is known for both its colonial era laws, which forbid homosexuality, and its iconic Pink Dot Festival, which celebrates the LGBT community. It has been governed through soft-authoritarian dominant-party rule since independence in 1965, by the People's Action Party (PAP), under conditions that make dissent and advocacy for change extremely challenging. The public emergence of the LGBT community, and particularly its gradual acceptance by authorities, is thus notable. That change has not extended to law reform, however, and Section 377A of the Penal Code, the law inherited from the British that criminalises homosexuality, remains. The government refuses to remove this law, preferring instead to retain it as an element in its broader apparatus of social control. Successive attempts to challenge these laws in the courts on constitutional grounds have also met with frustration, as discussed later in this Element.

While the city-state's leaders hold to their conservative mores and paternalistic politics, the electorate appears to be getting restless. The ruling party performed particularly badly in the 2020 general election, in significant contrast to the 2015 election, itself a surprisingly good result after a poor showing in 2011. The year 2020 saw a critical drop in the PAP's popular vote, widely interpreted as a failure to capture a strong mandate. The poor performance of Prime Minister Lee Hsien Loong's designated successor, Heng Swee Keat, threw leadership succession into doubt, and the government officially recognised an opposition leader for the first time (Pritam Singh), giving unprecedented political legitimacy to an alternative vision. Young voters in particular clearly favour both more checks and balances against government, but also more diversity, and the opportunity to have frank public conversations about sensitive political issues (Walden 2020) – including sexuality and gender, as well as race, religion and class.

The government's continuing position, however, is that Singaporean society is socially conservative; that it has a responsibility to uphold social norms and values in this respect; and that the most appropriate way to do this is to leave Section 377A in place, while pursuing a publicised policy of non-enforcement. Somewhat disingenuously, the government suggests that this approach meets a range of competing desiderata. These include satisfying conservative religious and community leaders, allowing social space for the LGBT community, and sustaining a social environment that will attract those workers needed for Singapore's economic policy (Weiss 2007). The fortunes of SOGIESC rights claiming as a mode of political participation in Singapore are deeply imbricated with government management of these competing goals.

Prime Minister Lee Hsien Loong speaks of an 'uneasy compromise' for a society which 'is not that liberal on these matters' (Geddie 2020). Asked specifically about the possibility of change, to attract LGBT expats to Singapore, he responded, 'I think we are open, you know our rules in Singapore. No matter your sexual orientation, you're welcome to come work in Singapore. . . . [377A] remains on our legislation and it will for some time, but it has not inhibited people from living here' (Gorey 2019). Notwithstanding this 'welcome', the government's view remains that Singapore is 'not ready' for rights such as same-sex relationship recognition (Velasquez 2015). Rather, as Singapore's first Prime Minster Lee Kuan Yew said in 1998 when first broaching the topic of relaxing but not removing controls, 'what we are doing as a government is to leave people to live their own lives so long as they don't impinge on other people' (Tan n.d.b).

Systemic Discrimination and Exclusion

While the government argues that it welcomes LGBT people (workers, specifically), and does not discriminate against or harass them, in fact, it supports and upholds a governance structure of systematic disadvantage. Civil society groups engaged with the UN's Universal Periodic Review process (a form of rights claiming discussed in detail in the next section) used a submission there to argue that the continued existence of Section 377A serves 'to deny or uphold a wider range of discriminatory policies that effectively strip LGBT Singaporeans of many of the prerogatives and protections of citizenship' (Oogachaga and Pink Dot 2016, 1). Even when agencies or actors within the government see an opportunity to support the community, it can be very difficult to proceed, given that the undergirding normative orientation of the law repudiates such motivations.

To grasp this fully, it is important to understand that Section 377A is not an isolated section of the law but is the symbolic key to a broader regime. A critical place to examine this is in the nexus between the government's claim to be channelling and respecting the conservative moral norms of the population when it comes to sexuality and gender, on the one hand, and the extensive power it exercises to shape and constrain what those norms might be, and how they might be allowed to develop, on the other. The regulation of free-to-air radio and television, for example, is a principal instrument the government uses to shape public perceptions and attitudes. The codes governing these industries explicitly prohibit the broadcast of material that might be construed to 'promote, justify or glamorise' the 'lifestyles' of LGBT people (Oogachaga and Pink Dot 2016, 1).

Another legislative platform that takes its cues from the government's determination to retain, although not proactively enforce, Section 377A is the Societies Act, which has been used to deny LGBT people freedom and right of association and assembly. The Singaporean government deploys the Societies Act to regulate non-commercial associations. The registrar must be satisfied that an organisation's objectives are not contrary to the national interest. In denying the registration of LGBT groups, the registrar has argued that it is 'contrary to public interest to grant legitimacy to the promotion of homosexual activities and viewpoints' (Oogachaga and Pink Dot 2016, 2). Civil society groups contest the outcome, on the basis that a refusal to allow organisation hinders the provision of support and protection services to LGBT community members, who face discrimination and are in need of protection – a seemingly reasonable request of a government that claims to welcome LGBT people. The difficulty, of course, is that the national interest, as expressed in the law through Section 377A, continues to revile homosexuality, leaving the LGBT community no secure formal grounds for redress, nor any platform from which to materially extend the government's 'welcome' of LGBT people within society more broadly.

The fundamental conflict that we can see operating in the context of the Societies Act permeates the broader range of services, programmes and provisions that are conventionally understood to be the responsibilities of a government with respect to citizens and residents. Across the portfolios of Education and Youth Services, Health and Employment/Workplace protections, there are specific needs and concerns that relate to LGBT populations. These include, but are not limited to, bullying in schools, social exclusion and violence, harassment, mental health, depression, sexual health (including HIV/AIDS), provision of sex reassignment surgery, gender markers, so-called conversion therapy, workplace discrimination, fair employment treatment and diversity in employment.

While the government refuses to decriminalise homosexuality or systematically address matters of discrimination based on sexuality and gender, it has recognised the need to assure community members of their protection under the law – especially in a context of increased religiously motivated pushback, such as the Pink Dot Festival has experienced. In 2019, the government implemented changes to Singapore's religious harmony laws – mainly driven by the impact of social media and concerns about foreign interference. A new Explanatory Statement added to the Maintenance of Religious Harmony Act (MRHA) in 2019 explicitly includes among protected target groups those that share a non-normative sexual orientation. While neither the MRHA broadly nor the new statement provides additional protections, they do explicitly signal a commitment to protection under the law. SOGIESC rights advocates take this amendment as a clear signal that the government recognises that LGBT people have been targeted by violence that is religiously motivated – a 'momentous and significant' recognition (Tan n.d.a).

Legal Reform

Legal mobilisation has been a central feature of LGBT activism in Singapore. As Lynette Chua puts it, 'From the movement's timorous beginnings to its coming out, activists continued to interact with formal law and the political norms of legal legitimacy as important factors that shape their tactics' (Chua 2014, 151). This interaction is embedded in what Chua theorises as the *pragmatic resistance* which characterises the pursuit of LGBT freedoms and rights under soft authoritarian rule in Singapore. More so than elsewhere in the region, this engagement with the law has been a feature of contestation; critical to its success, in Chua's analysis, has been the capacity to use both the relative autonomy and the cultural power of the law, in choosing the tactics that will advance the movement.

Efforts to repeal Section 377A exemplify this approach, with a campaign in 2007 marking the LGBT movement's 'coming out' in Singapore (Chua 2014). A government review of the Penal Code offered an opening: the LGBT community seized the opportunity to challenge their legal marginalisation by presenting a parliamentary petition. The review did lead the government to reform the code, but it chose only to repeal portions of Section 377 that dealt with sexual conduct 'against the order of nature' between heterosexual persons (oral and anal sex). As discussed earlier in this Element, it left Section 377A, dealing with 'gross indecency' between men, on the books, while making it clear that it would not enforce the law.

However, within a few years the law *was* enforced. In 2010, police caught Tan Eng Hong in a public toilet engaged in an act of 'gross indecency'. He was initially charged under Section 377A. Tan went to the courts, challenging the constitutionality of Section 377A in relation to rights to life and liberty, equal protection and freedom of association. A series of cases ensued during which additional plaintiffs, Lim Meng Suang and Kenneth Chee Mun-Leon, also brought challenges to Section 377A. Singapore's court of last resort, the Court of Appeal, considered these challenges collectively in 2014, and dismissed them (HDT n.d.).

Section 377A was thrown into the spotlight again in 2018 after the Indian Supreme Court decided to repeal its Section 377 laws, which also criminalised homosexuality. Singapore's LGBT community organised a campaign to deliver a '#ready4repeal' petition to Parliament. In a move that mirrored the previous decade's initial debates on Section 377A, they presented the petition to Parliament in the course of a public consultation on the Penal Code – although the government had already indicated that Section 377A was not up for consideration.

This also provided the impetus for another wave of constitutional challenges in an environment of considerable public support. By the end of the following year, three separate challenges had been filed with the High Court, by Dr Roy Tan Seng Kee (a general practitioner and LGBT activist), Johnson Ong Ming (a DJ) and Bryan Choong (former director of Oogachaga, an LGBT organisation). Once again, the arguments presented dealt with questions of equality, personal liberty, freedom of expression and equal protection, as well as the standing of pre-colonial laws and the policy of non-enforcement. Senior figures came out in support of these arguments; the former chief justice and attorney general Chan Sek Keong published a legal analysis clearly detailing the case that Section 377A was unconstitutional (Chan 2019). Expectations were high for a different outcome than in 2014.

In March 2020, however, the High Court ruled that Section 377A *was* constitutional and would be retained, saying that the arguments presented had not swayed the Court or provided reasons for it to depart from the earlier binding decision of the Court of Appeal (Kurohi 2020). The Court continues to support the government's approach with respect to the non-enforcement of the law: that – as we saw above – Singapore is a conservative society, 'not ready', in PM Lee's words, to decriminalise homosexuality. As Justice See Kee Oon expressed it, 'Statutory provisions serve an important role in reflecting public sentiment and beliefs. Section 377A, in particular, serves the purpose of safeguarding public morality by showing societal moral disapproval of male homosexual acts' (Sim 2020). The three men who brought the new cases to the High Court are appealing the decision (Lam 2021; Lum 2021).

Pink Dot: 'We Are Ready'

The Pink Dot Festival is an annual celebration of the LGBT community, in which a sea of pink transfigures Hong Lim Park, the site of Singapore's Speakers' Corner, the country's only designated venue for protests. It is the most obvious form of broad *social* participation on SOGIESC matters; its transition to a node for *political* participation, as a form of rights claiming, is a key part of the story. From 2,500 people who attended in 2009, numbers swelled tenfold over the next decade, a remarkable achievement given Singapore's legal and cultural constraints on protest. Indeed, for much of its history, and in keeping with the Singaporean LGBT movement's cautious pragmatism (Chua 2014), Pink Dot designated itself a family-friendly 'event' held in support of the LGBT community – not a conventional pride parade, nor a political protest.

In recent years, however, as the popularity of the festival has surged, and frustration with repeatedly stymied legal reform has grown, the event has taken on a distinctly more political hue. By the mid-2010s, Pink Dot's increasingly established presence was generating political contestation in various domains. The year 2014 saw opposition from right-wing and conservative religious groups (Muslim and Christian) manifest itself in the form of the counter-protest 'Wear White' movement, a visible demonstration of the background US-style culture war based around the sanctity of the family, that had also been building for some time in Singapore (Weiss 2013). In 2016, Pink Dot itself provided placards on which citizens and permanent residents (but not foreigners, to comply with Singapore law) could articulate more protest-oriented messages. For its part, the government altered regulations to prevent foreign sponsorship of Pink Dot – denying critical financial support the event previously received from big names such as Apple and Google. In 2017, the government further prohibited foreigners from being physically present in Hong Lim Park during Pink Dot. Singaporeans rallied to the cause in response, both turning out in record numbers and launching a 'Red Dot for Pink Dot' (referring to Singapore's 'little red dot' moniker) fund-raising campaign from local businesses. In 2018, in response to the prime minister's claim that Singapore was not ready for law reform, the Pink Dot light display included the words 'We Are Ready.' The political edge to the movement was becoming sharper (Han and Ho 2020b).

This became manifest directly from the stage during 2019's Pink Dot. With legal reform in India and fresh challenges lodged with Singapore's High Court, many LGBT Singaporeans, including event host Paerin Choa, had been angered by comments from Prime Minister Lee Hsien Long. Citing the success of Pink Dot, Lee had argued that LGBT people were not 'inhibited' in Singapore. On the contrary, Choa argued from the stage, 'Prime Minister Lee, because of Section 377A, we are made invisible. . . . Because of Section 377A, we continue to be marginalised and we lead incomplete lives. Because of Section 377A, we deal with discrimination every day' – before leading the crowd in a chat: 'Tear. Down. This. Law! Tear. Down. This. Law!' (Han and Ho 2020a). Later, interspersed among the pink lights that formed the eponymous 'dot' were white lights which spelled out 'REPEAL 377A'. Throughout the event, the host reiterated, 'This is a protest' – not just a picnic (Han and Ho 2020b).

While it was not possible to hold Pink Dot in person during the COVID-19 pandemic, online versions of the event went ahead. In the legal domain, Section 377A challenges are ongoing, and other forms of discrimination have also driven protest, amplifying public attention. In 2021, youths protesting the treatment of transgender school students assembled and were arrested outside the Ministry of Education; they believed they had no choice but to put themselves at risk in order to be heard (TOC 2021). A new generation may not be satisfied with the existing compromise, but they face an uphill battle. Prevailing social attitudes remain conservative, despite incremental change, and the government remains unwilling to adjust legal parameters. While the government is prepared to give ground at times for practical and utilitarian reasons, full formal political participation as a matter of right is out of reach for Singapore's queers for as long as authorities sustain an ideology of social control centred on the retention of Section 377A.

Thailand

Bangkok is reputed to be the 'gay capital' of Southeast Asia, a queer paradise in a country with the broadest tolerance for varieties of sexuality and gender diversity in the region. Thailand's kathoeys, ladyboys, toms and dees and gays are only the most well-known of a proliferation of identities that blend elements of masculinity and femininity (Sinnott 2004). The living presence of a wide range of these queer identities, subjectivities and the cultures they create is visible in the urban landscape of Bangkok and a variety of other Thai locales – Chiang Mai, Pattaya, Phuket. The intersection of sexuality and gender diversity with bourgeoning capitalism, international tourism (including medical tourism), the sex industry and the mediatisation and commodification of LGBTQ life in Thailand has been fertile ground for the proliferation of queer ways of being in the world (Jackson 2011). In the major population centres, a wide range of commercial venues caters for entertainments and services of all kinds, from bars, clubs, theatres and saunas to surgical reconstruction. Patrons can openly engage the opportunities afforded, knowing that the state offers no legal sanction. Thailand has enacted gender non-discrimination legislation and seemed till recently in the race to be among Asia's first jurisdictions to provide same-sex marriage, developments that burnish its reputation and progressive queer credentials.

However, the depiction of Thailand as a paradise for queers is as utopic here as it is anywhere else. The aforementioned account, while true, is partial: it emphasises the opportunities and experiences of visitors but elides much in the lived realities of queer people and communities within Thailand. While

Thailand is imagined as an exotic getaway for the Global North, and functions as a safe haven in the circuit of regionally mobile Asians queers, the experience of residents differs. Despite the glittering presence of the scene on the street, social sanctions against non-normative sexuality and gender display are widespread and discriminatory. Especially given the economic precarity, which commonly accompanies work and sociality for those who do not pass within established gender conventions, the scope for formal and informal rights claiming, to ensure the government both provides and protects those rights, remains extensive. The discussion below traces the contemporary status of sexuality and gender diversity rights provisions by following three current developments: the debate about legal recognition for same-sex relationships, a gender discrimination bill and shifts in societal attitudes of tolerance and inclusion.

Legal Recognition of Same-Sex Relationships

In July 2020, Thailand took a major step towards legally recognising and protecting same-sex relationships: the nation's Cabinet approved a Civil Partnership Bill, meaning that it could now progress to Parliament for debate and if passed, become law. The bill would grant recognition and registration of same-sex unions, allow adoption, and provide for inheritance and joint property ownership rights (CNA 2020).

Many in the LGBTQ community are not satisfied with the Civil Partnership Bill, however, and it has a competitor: an alternative proposal from the Move Forward Party (MFP, previously named the Future Forward Party). Whereas the Ministry of Justice's Civil Partnership Bill creates a new category of legally recognised relationship, the civil partnership, the Move Forward Party argues that a much better solution is simply to amend the existing marriage law to allow any two people to marry – regardless of their sex or gender. Tunyawaj Kamolwongwat, a Member of Parliament from the Move Forward Party, says: 'By amending the existing law on marriage, the rights afforded to opposite-sex couples will be extended. This will then allow people of any sex to marry. It's the right solution, given that every citizen must use the same law and the same standard. This is equality' (Promchertchoo 2020).

Tanwarin Sukkhapisit, Thailand's first transgender Member of Parliament, elected in 2019, is also a member of the MFP. Tanwarin is a campaigner for gender equality, and despite disagreeing with the Cabinet-backed proposal, appreciates the debate the competing proposals have generated for raising awareness in the general community, where ignorance and discrimination remain significant problems. While acknowledging the benefits that accrue from acknowledging civil unions, Tanwarin argues that such a law, nonetheless, 'misses the target'. Rather than producing equality before the law for all citizens – the constitutional standard – it produces different categories of legally recognised 'unions' with differential rights. They insist, 'If we are all equal as humans, then we should all enjoy the same basic rights and privileges under the same laws. Why create a separate marriage law for LGBT+ when we could just amend existing marriage laws to apply to all persons regardless of gender and sexuality?' (The Isaan Record 2019).

As Douglas Sanders shows, this debate has a long history among Thai same-sex marriage activists and proponents (Sanders 2019). On the one hand, a consensus exists that steps need to be taken to provide for relationship recognition. On the other hand, there has been significant disagreement – at times publicly acrimonious – about whether some form of separate registration system could satisfy immediate demands, given the constraints of a broader conservatively oriented social and political setting, or whether advocates should settle for nothing less than the same procedures and standards as apply to heterosexuals.

Earlier efforts at reform and bill-drafting consistently ran short of time, with proposals being upended by procedural timelines, elections, military coups. Most recently (November 2021), Thailand's Constitutional Court has ruled that existing marriage regulations, which stipulate that marriage is between a man and a woman, are not unconstitutional. Firmly supporting the existing law, the court argued that marriage equality would overturn the natural order and undermine the foundations of social order. In the midst of this disappointment, however, activists see a silver lining: after a decade of debate and stalled action, same-sex relationship recognition has a higher profile, a larger degree of community support, and a policy establishment that has come to view some degree of law reform as necessary.

Gender Discrimination

Thailand's Gender Equality Act, passed by Parliament in March of 2015 and implemented six months later, is the first of its kind in Southeast Asia. It outlaws 'unfair gender discrimination', where this means any act or omission 'which causes division, discrimination or limitation of any right and benefit either directly or indirectly without justification due to the fact that the person is male or female or of a different appearance from his/her own sex by birth' (Section 3 of the Act). In the words of the Act, what inspired it was the lack of a 'clear measure to prevent unfair gender discrimination … resulting in no protection and no appropriate fairness for those who are subject to unfair gender discrimination'.

The Act has been lauded for its progressive nature, and in particular for addressing discrimination against trans people. Nevertheless, the general assessment is that its weaknesses have made it a difficult tool to utilise, and that without other supporting legislation and attitudinal change in society at large, progress will remain limited. Among the weaknesses are exemptions for national security and religion. Significantly, any redress under the Act requires an aggrieved party. With this requirement, the Act runs into the characteristic difficulty those suffering discrimination face: 'Victims of gender discrimination have to be the ones reporting complaints themselves, and many are afraid to do so for fear of risking their education or career' (Subpawanthanakun 2017). Journalist Kornkritch Somjittranuki suggests that the advent of the law under a military government during a time of stifled free speech, perhaps in an effort to burnish its international human rights reputation, has limited local awareness of the opportunities it affords (Sinen 2017). One recent high-profile win under the law has been the case of Jirapat, a trans student at Chulalongkorn University. With support from activist Nada Chaiyajit, who had previously won a petition against the University of Phayao to have documents issued according to chosen gender as a matter of right (Thomson Reuters 2017), the case established that students could dress according to their gender identity (Prachatai 2019b). While positive, these steps represent incremental gains. Transgender teaching students, for example, report many instances of being rejected by schools for placement, and of universities offering inadequate support against such discrimination (Prachatai 2019a).

A case like this is significant for another reason, one which picks up inadequacies in Thailand's legal system, which go beyond the terms of the Gender Equality Act. While the Act may help provide redress against discrimination, the law must be able to see you – and to see you in a non-discriminatory manner – to have traction, so, '[i]t is no easy task to apply an anti-discrimination law to support an LGBTI population that is not legally recognised' (Muna-McQuay 2017). For trans people, the Equality Act is only one piece of the puzzle. Its guarantees around discrimination can only function if trans people are granted full legal status and recognition. At the moment, however, trans people (with or without genital surgery and notwithstanding sex/gender presentation) are unable to change their sex and gender markers on official documentation (Prachatai 2019b; Sanders 2020a, 346). The absence of a legal remedy sustains opportunities for discrimination in society (Mirtha 2017). There is no standard for how schools should treat transgender teachers, for example, and no protection against discrimination for them. In a different domain, transgender people held within correctional institutions are generally mis-gendered, denied hormone therapies and other medical services and frequently endure other depredations (Mahavongtrakul 2019). Another critical state institution, the military, requires that all males aged twenty must report for a lottery-based service draft. The law exempts those who have undergone genital surgery. However, until recently the exemption was attributed to a permanent mental disorder. After sustained legal action, a change of practice in 2011 led to the attribution of 'gender identity disorder', indicating instead a mismatch between a person's gender and their sex as identified at birth (Sanders 2020a, 346). Each of these different cases illustrates the need for a universal legal resolution, one which dovetails with the Gender Equality Act to ensure both legal recognition and protection against discrimination.

In response, local advocates are pursuing rights-based domestic remedies: a range of trans organisations are campaigning for a new law to protect their rights, seeking signatures from members of the public to launch it into formal parliamentary processes. The law would address trans people's 'name and title, marriage rights, military conscription and being treated as their gender in correctional facilities' (Glauert 2019; cf. Boonlert 2020).

Tolerance, Not Acceptance

In contrast to many other societies, where Western colonialism left a legacy of criminal sanctions on same-sex behaviour, in Thailand, which was not formerly colonised by any Western state, colonialism's primary impact for sexuality and gender minorities was the intensification of the masculine–feminine gender binary. As Jackson explains, beginning initially under absolute monarchy in the nineteenth century and then coming to be enforced mid-twentieth century, a gender ideology that mandated 'real men and true women' became normative, and translated into 'new bourgeois social attitudes of the proper man as the breadwinner of the family and the proper woman as a stay-at-home child-caring housewife'. Crossing these norms 'became something distasteful and disapproved of, regarded as a sign of a lack of "civilisation"' (Jackson 2013, 18–19; cf. Jackson 2003).

Today, while there is widespread public support for Thailand's queer communities, there is also continued stigma and discrimination, in particular for people who cross norms associated with masculinity and femininity. A recent study of social attitudes by the UNDP shows these patterns clearly, noting broad favourable attitudes and support for rights, but also reluctance towards having LGBT people as family members (UNDP 2019, 20–21). The report conveys the restrictive nature of social tolerance queer people face as they negotiate social expectations around 'appropriateness' (*mo-som*) and 'time-and-place' (*ka-la-the-sa*), expectations which constrain their capacity to live open and honest lives in day-to-day settings: with family, at work, in school and at university. The report elaborates, 'In these environments, LGBT people are told to hide who they are and pretend that they are not LGBT. A lesser form of this demand occurs when LGBT people are told to downplay their identity enough so that others can disregard it' (UNDP 2019, 31). Visible disregard for the gender binary, such as by effeminate gay men or masculine lesbians, generates social condemnation, including within the gay community, and socio-economic and religious backgrounds also filter and shape stigma in particular ways, in line with familial reputation, class status and religious dogma. A general societal taboo against discussion of sexuality, and a tendency for the media to represent LGBT persons as threats (for instance, as carriers of HIV), jokes or criminal elements, also contribute to continued stigmatisation and marginalisation.

SOGIESC advocates within Thai society have been at the forefront of pushing rights-based social and legal reforms in the region. While these efforts respond to local conditions, advocates routinely frame them in terms of an international SOGIESC rights claiming discourse – particularly for relationship recognition, anti-discrimination and trans-rights cases. Relative success in these campaigns enhances Thailand's image as a haven for queers, but this should not obscure the challenges of continued social and legal reform ahead.

Notwithstanding the differences between each of the five national cases we have examined, SOGIESC rights have emerged as a mechanism for political participation, and have played an important (if differentiated) role in activists' and advocates' strategies as they grapple with their local political contexts. These contexts, in turn, appear to be moving along divergent trajectories. In Indonesia and Malaysia in particular, the situation appears increasingly fraught, while in the Philippines, Singapore and Thailand, various forms of progress mix with entrenched discriminations and social prejudice. While the legal and political standing of SOGIESC rights across the five nations varies significantly, the language and advocacy modes of rights claiming have become increasingly ubiquitous – facilitated in part by interaction between activist communities, international trends and the development within the region of its own human rights regime. In the next section, we move from national narratives to a perspective informed by regional SOGIESC organising within a human rights frame. Starting from the very local experience of communal support in the face of violence and discrimination, this relational and interpersonal activity can, in its solidaristic dimensions, become a potent form of rights-based political participation. We turn to examine how this has transpired in tandem with the development of the broader human rights architecture of the region, to further explore SOGIESC rights claiming as a mode of political participation.

4 Civil Society and Rights Advocacy

Civil society organisations across Southeast Asia have been the principal drivers of regional SOGIESC rights claiming, developing relationships, networks, strategies and platforms which enable that political engagement. As we see in this section, this work starts with community support at the interpersonal level – rights abuse is by definition local, impacting individuals and their communities. We follow the chain of rights organising from such communal solidarism to national and regional organising, and examine engagement with formal governmental rights regimes, both in ASEAN and at the global level via the UN. The patterns we observe illustrate the key distinctive features of rights claiming as a mode of political participation: it depends on linkages across different scales, from the local to the global; and works across normative, political and organisational domains. It is the combination of these elements which gives rights claiming its force and efficacy. The contemporary visibility and impact of SOGIESC rights claiming in the region have emerged as these discreet elements have come together in various constellations of solidaristic and emancipatory activity.

Local, National and Regional Organising

Often marginalised, subject to discrimination, violence and intimidation, and disenfranchised economically and politically, sexuality and gender diverse people depend on community support in their local environments. At the personal level, community members provide for one another when income is taken away, support one another when rejected by family and friends, grieve together after brutal assault and murder and collectively source medical assistance. Social networks pull together to privately organise housing, emergency shelter, health and financial support for those excluded from other forms of social support. Such networks are critical, as shown, for example, by current events in Malaysia and Indonesia, where renewed government persecution (Malaysia), social violence (Indonesia) and the COVID-19 pandemic exacerbate levels of precarity (Afifi 2021; Rodriguez and Suvianita 2020; Sutrisno 2020). As Lini Zurlia from the ASEAN SOGIE Caucus puts it:

> The most powerful thing we can do as LGBT individuals in Indonesia is to build a collective, a community, to find a support system. Out of this collective, we work together to build a safety mechanism to protect ourselves. When we experience violence, what should we do? We must do these things alone and forget, even just for a while, that we are actually citizens of this country. (Partogi 2021)

While groups do form and organise, they also experience resistance, opposition and refusal. The extent and character of this pushback varies according to political and social context, and sometimes despite progress in advancing formal protection regimes. Common experiences include intimidation, the interruption or forced cancellation of events, the targeting of dissent by agents of the state, threats of and actual violence, police brutality, punitive legal measures, imprisonment, the spread of false and misleading information, the mobilisation of identity politics associated with so-called traditional values and the spread of stigma, bullying and discriminatory action.

The fundamental question of *how* to organise, when the state in which you live either specifically criminalises your existence or has a more general aversion to political dissent, is a continual challenge (ASC 2021b). In most Southeast Asian states, including those examined earlier, forms of open organising, however constrained, can be maintained. In a few, informal or even clandestine organising may be necessary – with Brunei the most extreme case. Establishing and registering a formal organisation can be a fraught process (increasingly difficult in Indonesia, for example), but is commonly helpful for legal or financial reasons.

Sexuality and gender diverse groups have established civil society organisations in most Southeast Asian states. How they came into being, and the particular emphases of their work and advocacy, speak to the variable forms of political participation, representation, contestation of public policy, social awareness and protest across the region. The political spaces in which these organisations operate are diverse, with differing levels of freedom and constraint, determined by domestic political conditions. Among the organisations that form, priorities and purposes also shape who participates and to what end. While coalitional work is a constant feature of the organising landscape, there is also a significant measure of contestation and dispute. Needs and interests among groups do not always harmoniously align; the capacity, desire and freedom to engage in overtly political challenges raises continuous tension.

In the Philippines, for example, organising can be relatively straightforward – as we saw, the Philippines is famous for its gay political party, Ladlad (Pascual 2012), and is home to a multitude of other queer organisations. In Indonesia, notwithstanding the current 'LGBT' moral panic playing out at the national level, there are many local organisations across the archipelago, providing a wide range of services and functions for sexuality and gender diverse communities (ASC 2021b; Khanis 2013). In Malaysia, the queer and trans communities have dense networks of communication and support, despite increased levels of governmental suppression aided by a resurgent religious right (Sulathireh 2021). The dynamic is different in Vietnam, where organising is constrained not by the criminalisation of homosexuality, but by governmental antipathy to any kind of *political* dissent, reinforced by recurrent harsh crackdowns. A similar dynamic operates in Cambodia, where general political repression and widespread discrimination, rather than illegality, shape the lived experience of the queer community (APCOM 2017; Pisey, Heng, and Low 2019). In Brunei, the most restrictive state in the region, grassroots organising is of necessity informal and under the radar (Abdul 2018; Black 2019; Destination Justice 2018; Teik 2019). By contrast, in tightly regulated Singapore, where, as examined earlier, there is continued criminalisation, the LGBTIQ community has a visible and open presence won through decades of what we saw Chua describe as *pragmatic resistance*. Activists avoid breaking the law, but push against normative limits, adjusting nimbly to pressures as they seek to mobilise community, challenge the state and address movement opponents (Chua 2014, 5).

Thailand's reputation as a regional queer haven is countered by the impact of military government and democratic retrenchment, along with widespread discrimination; at the same time, young queer activists were significant participants in the pro-democracy street protests of 2020 (Jommaroeng 2021; Sanders 2020b). This participation points to a critical aspect of civil society organising across the region: its intersectional nature. A wide range of allied civil society organisations support LGBTIQ advocacy, and queer organisations across the region reciprocate through broad solidaristic advocacy, with some also pushing for more radical and alternative forms of emancipatory regional organising (cf. Aban and Sy 2020). Political repression, poverty, access to work, gender equality, exploitation in the workplace, the treatment of migrant workers, human trafficking, extrajudicial killing, digital tracking and surveillance and a wide range of other issues around which civil society organises are of concern to and impact upon sexuality and gender diverse people.

This dynamic is clearly on display in the origins of the ASEAN SOGIE Caucus (ASC), a key regional umbrella organisation for advocacy and activism. Emerging out of the ASEAN Civil Society Conference (ACSC) of the ASEAN People's Forum (APF), ASC was established in 2011. The previous year's Conference Statement had included SOGIE demands, calling upon ASEAN member states to repeal laws which criminalise SOGIE, either directly or indirectly; to promote the equal rights of LGBTIQ people; and to de-pathologise SOGIE and instead promote measures for psycho-social well-being (ACSC/APF 2011). These demands were in part precipitated by Islamist vigilantes' having interrupted and shut down the 2010 ILGA (then International Lesbian and Gay Association) Asia conference in Surabaya (cf. Liang 2010).

The establishment of ASC created a distinctive regional voice for SOGIESC advocates, self-consciously addressed to ASEAN and its member states, covering a wide range of solidaristic concerns (Langlois 2014; Langlois et al. 2017; Weiss 2021), with a particular focus on the inclusion of SOGIESC matters in human rights mandates (ASC 2021a, 4). Its emergence out of and continuing relationship with the ACSC/APF means that ASC is regional in its core DNA. In contrast to international LGBTIQ organisations which generally arrive as outposts from the Global North, ASC's advocacy and activism are positioned entirely within Southeast Asia, giving a driving edge to its political critique. It is headquartered and has a secretariat in Quezon City, Philippines, with key officers also resident in Indonesia and Vietnam. It is unique among SOGIESC organisations in highlighting its regional identity by using 'ASEAN' in its own name, and has a history of engaging with ASEAN's own region-wide identity formation projects in order to visibilise the queer community – such as through innovative uses of social media and video online (ASC 2015). Equally important is the formative environment out of which ASC emerged as an organisation: it was cross-sectoral, intersectional and solidaristic. Unlike the many national and regional organisations that have health and HIV/AIDS as their operational raison d'être – not infrequently the only feasible premise on which to establish and sustain a sanctioned formal organisation – the orientation of ASC has been overtly political and activist since its inception, affording it a distinctive role and voice in the regional landscape of SOGIE organising (Castañeda 2020; Muntarbhorn 2021; Nguyen 2020; Poonkasetwattana 2021; Silverio 2020; Zurlia 2020).

A significant number of other international organisations involved with SOGIESC advocacy operate in the region, mainly based out of Bangkok. These include international NGOs that have global reach, intergovernmental agencies which run SOGIESC-related programmes, regional organisations with a health or HIV/AIDS focus, diplomatic missions from (primarily) Global North states and a range of other supportive research and commercial entities. The UNDP, with its 'Being LGBTIQ in Asia' initiative (established in 2014), is perhaps the highest-profile agency to have offered a comprehensive capacity building and research programme across the region. The programme's stated objectives include: '[i]ncreased participation of LGBTI people in policy development including universal access to health, social services, education and employment, and rule of law and accountability mechanisms' and '[g]reater understanding amongst stakeholders of the development dimensions and inclusion of people of diverse sexual orientation and gender identities' (UNDP n.d.). ILGA Asia, similarly, has its secretariat in Bangkok, where it operates as the regional arm of ILGA World. ILGA Asia is comprised of over 100 organisations from the broader Asian region, including members from each Southeast Asian state. It hosts a regional conference bi-annually, and in its training, advocacy and capacity building work is primarily oriented around the formal international human rights regime anchored in UN conventions and covenants. The Asia Pacific Transgender Network (APTN) is also based in Bangkok. APTN is a trans-led advocacy organisation that operates across five domains: movement building, advocacy, leadership development, public campaigning and research. Bangkok was the site, too, of the first Asian Intersex forum in 2018, leading to the establishment of Intersex Asia, an intersex-led organisation established to promote the human rights of intersex people in Asia (based in Taiwan). Other NGOs, such as OutRight Action International, have personnel located in other states in the region (such as Singapore and the Philippines), and also engage in research, monitoring and advocacy work.

APCOM, the Asia-Pacific Coalition on Male Sexual Health, was founded in 2007 and moved to Bangkok in 2012. It is a HIV/health-related organisation that has found it increasingly advantageous to articulate its work explicitly through human rights frames and networks, illustrating the growing (and cross-sectoral) utility of rights claiming as a mode of participation. APCOM runs capacity building programmes for MSM (men who have sex with men) and transgender networks across the Asia-Pacific region, engages in community-led research around HIV services and engages in other activities to support SOGIESC communities. HIV prevention remains a major health focus for key populations of people with diverse SOGIESC. APCOM's purposeful embrace of a human rights focus dates from 2013–14, as part of a strategy to address the exclusion those most marginalised experience. Community-based organisations are central to the HIV response, but in order to function, they need governments to recognise them, which in turn is a problem if they cannot be seen or heard due to policy frameworks or social rejection. Engaging rights frameworks thus becomes a key factor in being able to maintain and advance community participation and population-led service delivery in health. APCOM has also rolled out a programme that focuses on inclusion rights in the workplace, with a strong focus on engaging the private sector as a venue for social change. While APCOM maintains a much lower political profile than comparatively radical organisations such as ASC, its utilisation of the rights agenda and SOGIESC rights claiming has become an integral part of both its advocacy and health-related work (APCOM 2020; Poonkasetwattana 2021).

Collectively, these international organisations and their peers provide a regional hub of networking, activity and organising. For activists and advocates they are a critical access point for expertise, resources, training, education and finance. In cooperation with local counterparts, they support an annual calendar of major international conferences, undertake comparative country studies and thematic research, assist engagement with the international human rights regime via UN mechanisms and facilitate diplomatic and intergovernmental interest, support and resourcing.

Advocacy Utilising Formal Human Rights Systems

It is only very recently that the international human rights regime has provided firm support for LGBTIQ human rights (Langlois 2019). The 1994 Toonen case at the UN, which addressed laws that criminalised sodomy in the Australian state of Tasmania, precipitated the shift (cf. Langford and Creamer 2017). UN instruments that address forms of discrimination have subsequently included sexual orientation. But this advance, won through litigation, did not truly represent uncompromising or systemic support. In a 2007 meeting, independent jurists, international lawyers, academics and activists, fed up with the slow pace of change, took matters into their own hands. They met in Yogyakarta, Indonesia, and from there argued that *current* human rights law, if it were applied, could protect LGBTIQ people. The meeting drafted a document that set out the ways in which human rights law – as it stood – offered these protections, making clear to practitioners and advocates how best to utilise *existing* legal provisions in LGBTIQ human rights advocacy. The Yogyakarta Principles, as they became known, galvanised a new turn to the international human rights regime as a resource for the protection of queer people (Brown 2010; O'Flaherty 2015; Waites 2009; Yogyakarta Principles 2007).

Within a decade, the HRC of the UN also demonstrated new interest and began regularly commissioning reports about violence and discrimination based upon sexual orientation and gender identity. The then Secretary General Ban Ki-Moon declared the struggle for the protection of LGBT rights 'one of the great, neglected challenges of our time' (UN 2013). This momentum culminated in the creation of a UN special procedure, the IE in Sexual Orientation and Gender Identity. The inaugural occupant of this role was Vitit Muntarbhorn from Thailand, a key figure behind the Yogyakarta Principles process. His appointment significantly heightened the profile of these issues in Southeast Asia (Muntarbhorn 2021). Support for the IE role from states in the region, however, was mixed. Of those belonging to the HRC, only Vietnam voted in favour, with Indonesia against and the Philippines abstaining. When the General Assembly voted on the matter, after an anti-LGBTIQ coalition attempted to scuttle the procedure, only Cambodia, Thailand and Timor-Leste joined Vietnam (UN 2016). When the IE procedure was renewed in 2019, the Philippines was the only regional state on the HRC, and rather than abstaining as in 2016, unexpectedly voted in favour (ARC International, ILGA World, and ISHR 2019).

During the period of these developments, the question of relationship recognition between same-sex partners had become a high-profile political and legal issue in a wide range of states, particularly in the Global North. Among LGBTIQ campaigners and human rights advocates alike, the ability of two people of the same sex to marry had become a cause célèbre. It had also become the leading edge of culture wars and ideological politics between conservatives and progressives, and a major touchstone for debates about democracy, human rights and Western neo-imperialism in large swathes of the Global South (Winter 2018). In Southeast Asia, as noted earlier, equal marriage has gained some positive traction in Thailand and Vietnam, although these remain the only states where any form of relationship recognition is even remotely likely in the near term (Jommaroeng 2021; Pham 2020); elsewhere it is a utopian hope, or a counter-productive culture-war distraction from immediate material needs.

The conjunction of a global SOGIESC human rights turn and the emergence of a human rights regime in ASEAN shape the form that SOGIESC rights claiming as a mode of political participation takes. As Southeast Asia develops its own human rights regime, wider transnational elements have textured the political landscape upon which what Gomez and Ramcharan call the 'nascent architecture for the protection of human rights' (2020, 2) is being built. This parallel evolution particularly strengthens the capacity to move from normative claims of political protest to the institutional engagement that comes with the formal recognition of specific claims. In this shift, the tripartite nature of the broader rights regime's 'nascent architecture' has been crucial, allowing advocates to argue for the transfer of recognition from one level to another.

The three institutional components of the regional rights architecture Gomez and Ramcharan identify speak to the international, regional and national elements of the international human rights regime, respectively. Internationally, the UN's HRC's establishment of a new process of Universal Periodic Review (since 2006) has been a critical development for accountability, but also for grassroots access to the global regime. At the regional level, we have the establishment of ASEAN's own human rights institutions, centred around the ASEAN Intergovernmental Commission on Human Rights (AICHR) and the ASEAN Human Rights Declaration (AHRD) (Langlois 2021; Langlois and Davies 2021). And across the region, five states have NHRIs that comply with the UN's Paris Principles regulating their independence (1993). Gomez and Ramcharan comment, 'The critical question is whether [these elements] individually or collectively provide protection of fundamental human rights.' Their overall assessment is that this function 'appears to be missing' (Gomez and Ramcharan 2020, 3, cf. 5). Whether omitted at the institution's creation (such as with AICHR) or eroded and obstructed by institutional revision and state behaviour (NHRIs and UPR), these institutions' capacity to investigate or constrain is limited. Nonetheless, SOGIESC advocates and civil society more broadly have vigorously engaged all of them, given their value to the pursuit of SOGIESC rights recognition and promotion, even if not (yet) effective in providing protection. We now examine each in turn.

Universal Periodic Review

The introduction of the UPR process into the UN human rights system in 2006 was a major innovation for holding states accountable to their human rights commitments. It provided a new set of tools for showing the presence of discrimination and violence against LGBTIQ people, and for pressing policy-makers to act in response. The essence of UPR is a cyclical review (every four to five years) of each state's human rights record by its peers. Each stage of the review process includes an opportunity for engagement and contribution from NGOs, making the process an attractive mechanism for access and visibility. Participants may submit written reports, which are archived within the UPR system, establishing a record of engagement against which action can be measured. NGOs can make oral statements for states' peer review, further amplifying the voice of grassroots advocates (e.g. ILGA 2017). It is worth noting that the initial UPR cycle coincided with the period in which the UN system turned its attention fully to LGBTI rights as human rights.

The opportunities UPR affords have been the site of considerable investment by Southeast Asian LGBTIQ NGOs, who have engaged together at the domestic level to gather information and write reports. Cross-movement collaboration has also been central (Chong 2020; Silverio 2020, 2021). LGBTIQ NGOs have strategised with other rights advocacy groups to find synergies and ensure maximum exposure for SOGIESC issues across a range of rights domains. The role of regional and international LGBTIQ human rights organisations with existing institutional connections and experience with the UN has been critical. ILGA-Asia, APCOM, Outright, ASEAN SOGIE Caucus and Destination Justice, among others, have played key roles in facilitating cooperation, offering training workshops for how to engage the UPR process, report writing, getting people to the UN to make statements, and diplomatic follow-up at home (e.g. APCOM 2016). These organisations also distribute and archive reports and recordings on their websites, providing a valuable resource for tracking and measuring social, legal and political change (ASC 2018; Destination Justice 2018; UNDP n.d.).

UPR has provided an unprecedented opening for queer people in the region to address their governments and policymakers, in a forum that recognises their claims and is designed to ensure voice and accountability. It is a precious opportunity for a community that is routinely silenced and criminalised at home. Notwithstanding this, effective participation in UPR requires extensive engagement with the institutional constellation of the human rights regime: global NGOs, diplomatic missions, the institutions of the UN. The constituent parts of this regime come with their own culture, politics, political economy and power dynamics.

In interviews undertaken for this project, respondents voiced a range of concerns in discussions of UPR, offered with some hesitation, lest they be thought to undercut work that was understood to be valuable, indeed critical. The importance of using UPR to get regional LGBTIQ rights issues on the table is a given, sometimes in conjunction with engaging other instruments. One such intersection is with the Convention on the Rights of the Child (CRC) (Chong 2020); the Philippines government, for instance, accepted a UPR recommendation on SOGIE violence in schools and the CRC reporting process itself has referenced SOGIE in observations on Singapore and Brunei (Silverio 2021). Notwithstanding this, some interviewees were concerned about the way in which the UPR and related rights processes 'discipline' participants. Intergovernmental institutions and international NGOs have formal and informal cultures of participation and professionalism; they necessarily have priorities and procedures that become manifest as they gather and curate data for formal presentation. The translation of complex, politically loaded community experiences and on-the-ground dynamics, which rarely have rights-based anchors, into the templates of the international human rights regime, can be a thankless and resource-intensive task. The expectations of international partners are not always aligned with the purposes of local and regional actors (Afifi 2021; Chong 2020; Cristobal 2020; Jommaroeng 2021; Silverio 2020; Sulathireh 2021).

Another set of responses concern the payoff: what outcomes has UPR delivered? Cambodian NGO Destination Justice has analysed the first two rounds of UPR, finding that the Philippines, Thailand and Vietnam appear significantly willing to act on UPR recommendations. Cambodia, Laos, Myanmar (pre-coup) and Timor-Leste were 'partially willing' to consider recommendations. By contrast, Brunei made 'no effort'; Indonesia 'consistently failed to address . . . oppression, discrimination, and violence'; Malaysia failed to address concerns; and Singapore 'acted slowly' on some counts and failed to address others. With the (then) exception of Myanmar, the states that criminalise homosexuality were most likely to prevaricate on action. While some states made general recommendations to one another, which *might* encompass LGBTIQ people *if* implemented, only a group of Western states, notably

Canada, France, Norway and Switzerland, made SOGIESC-specific recommendations (Destination Justice 2017, 102). Destination Justice observe that the pattern of responses over the first two cycles of UPR are a useful guide for how civil society might prepare for the next round.

However, it is at this point that questions about payoff start to become critical. There is little evidence of any direct link between UPR activity and relief for LGBTIQ people in their national political environments or in their local communities. In many jurisdictions across the region, the clear intention of governments is to either disregard the issue or exacerbate discrimination and violence by using 'the LGBTs' as a political football and cause for moral panic. Under these conditions, and notwithstanding the esteem in which UPR is held as a mechanism for holding states accountable, the cost–benefit analysis for engagement by community NGOs is pressing, both as a matter of resourcing, and more substantively, in strategic terms of what kinds of activities will generate on-the-ground, effective, practical help for communities (cf. Destination Justice 2018).

Regional Rights Mechanisms: ASEAN

At around the same time that the UN was instituting UPR, ASEAN made its radical pivot on human rights. This was a move from – variously – rejection, abuse, denial and indifference to institutional embrace and rhetorical enthusiasm. The rejection of human rights and democracy in the name of Asian values (Langlois 2001) was replaced with rights-based institution building. In 2009, the AICHR was inaugurated (Tan 2011). Shortly afterwards, in 2012, the AHRD was promulgated (Renshaw 2013). Other instruments have followed. The international human rights regime, long absent a regional counterpart in Asia, could now look to an ASEAN sub-regional institutional rights framework, complete with integration into the region's future planning: the flagship ASEAN Community Vision 2025 statement articulates a future direction which is rules-based, people-oriented and people-centred: one in which all enjoy democracy, good governance, human rights and fundamental freedoms (ASEAN Secretariat 2015).

Human rights advocates working with sexuality and gender diverse populations within ASEAN, however, have seen little benefit from this formal embrace of human rights. Indeed, the ASEAN rights regime fails to protect against discrimination based on sexuality and gender diversity. The exclusion of this ground from the AHRD was deliberate, a consequence of disagreement among state representatives. It is a clear demonstration of how 'the ASEAN way', the association's famous requirement for consensus among member states, drives low standards of protection. While representatives from the Philippines, Thailand and Indonesia were willing to incorporate sexuality rights in the Declaration, the governments of Singapore, Malaysia and Brunei directed their representatives to oppose (Langlois 2014, 312; Weiss 2021, 197). For ASEAN's pivot to human rights, the formal protection of sexuality and gender rights proved too much to ask.

For LGBTIQ community members across the region and their allies, ASEAN's response has been wholly inadequate. Their view – strongly bolstered by developments such as the Yogyakarta Principles and the UN's UPR – was that human rights necessarily included the rights of LGBTIQ people. Organisations across the region, prominent among them the ASEAN SOGIE Caucus, used ASEAN's turn to human rights to amplify their demands, gaining traction from the regional body's internal inconsistencies and failure to satisfy world-best-practice standards.

The final version of the AHRD excluded protection from discrimination on the basis of sexuality. This produced a stinging and often repeated rebuke from civil society: 'This [Declaration] not only shows a lack of respect to LGBTIQ people but also makes a mockery of the international human rights values and principles that all nations and citizens abide by and are held accountable to' (ASC 2012, para 1). Similar controversy surrounded the adoption of subsequent human rights instruments within ASEAN. The Declaration on the Elimination of Violence against Women and Children, like the AHRD, was shielded from civil society feedback, and in the end did not include references to sexuality. In a statement, the ASEAN SOGIE Caucus indicated deep concern about an emerging pattern of ASEAN human rights instruments excluding sexuality discrimination (ASC 2013).

Even after ASEAN shifted its orientation to use rights language and build rights institutions, the relationship between ASEAN's elite political leadership and the human rights advocacy community was still one of antagonism and opposition – on sexuality and gender rights, as on a range of other issues. Peak human rights lobby, ASIA-FORUM, evaluating the first decade of AICHR's performance, expressed unambiguously in a report the formal constraints on ASEAN's human rights institutions by their domestic political masters:

> As compared to other regional and international human rights mechanisms … the AICHR has by far the weakest protection record. The majority of the AICHR Representatives, as instructed by their governments, have consistently refused to implement even the limited protection mandate expressly conferred by its [Terms of Reference], let alone interpret the protection provisions creatively and progressively. The result has been a resounding silence of the AICHR on any human rights violations, in a decade that saw mass human rights violations, some of which – in

> Myanmar and the Philippines in particular – amounted to the worst crimes
> under international law. AICHR was equally silent in the face of continued
> repression of peaceful dissent and freedom of expression throughout
> the region, criminalisation of LGBTIQ and human rights defenders and
> repression of minorities, and numerous other human rights violations.
>
> (Hanara 2019, 42)

For many observers, this reticence came as no surprise, and might be thought to
warrant a dismissive attitude towards ASEAN's turn to human rights – confirm-
ation of the 'fig leaf' interpretation of the new regime (cf. Davies 2021). It is
worth noting, however, that while it is true that, as stated above, 'the majority'
of AICHR representatives appear constrained in their activities by political
imperatives, there have been some notable exceptions. Recent country representatives from Indonesia and Malaysia, in particular (Yuyun Wahyuningrum
and Eric Paulsen, respectively), are frequently seen facilitating access and
activity in civil society and have been noted as significant allies among
SOGIESC advocates (See Wahyuningrum in Gadong 2021). They have used
the limited scope of their office to the greatest possible extent, turning their
attention to extensive consultation with civil society, and making themselves
available to speak and engage on platforms that unambiguously critique elite
power; push for accountability, reform and genuine democratisation and seek to
end discrimination, including against LGBTIQ populations.

Incremental gains are possible here. While AICHR has no formal complaints mechanism, as Wahyuningrum has detailed, in November 2019,
'AICHR agreed that all incoming letters of complaint would be acknowledged
by the ASEAN Secretariat; and the letters would now be tabled in AICHR
meetings and then forwarded to the concerned country Representative to
AICHR. It is up to the relevant country Representative to address the complaint' (Wahyuningrum 2021). This process opens new possibilities for advocates to make, and have acknowledged, representations to AICHR on
SOGIESC matters. Indeed, in 2019, ASC, the International Commission on
Jurists, Forum Asia and Southeast Asia Press Alliance had already written to
AICHR with concerns over Brunei's Syariah Penal Code, with provisions that
constitute forms of torture and ill treatment, and which impact women,
children and SOGIE communities in particular (ASC 2019; Silverio 2019;
Zurlia 2020). While discretion in any action or follow-up lies with the AICHR
chair and the country representative, acknowledgement and documentation
are important milestones on the road to accountability. More generally, proponents of these changes consider this 'evolution' of AICHR's powers
a positive, incremental step towards more active protection capability
(Wahyuningrum 2021).

National Human Rights Institutions

While all ASEAN member states participate in the ASEAN human rights regime through AICHR and through their adoption of the AHRD, only a few have NHRIs, and not all of these meet the standards of independence and autonomy the United Nations articulates for such institutions – the Paris Principles (UN General Assembly 1993). The Philippines Commission on Human Rights, established in 1987, was the earliest NHRI in Southeast Asia. This was followed by Indonesia's Komisi Nasional Hak Asasi Manusia (Komnas HAM) in 1993, Malaysia's Suruhanjaya Hak Asasi Manusia Malaysia (SUHAKAM) in 2000 and the Thai Human Rights Commission (THRC) in 2001. The Myanmar National Human Rights Commission (MNHRC, established 2011) does not fully comply with the Paris Principles. These institutions are networked through the Asia Pacific Forum of NHRIs, which has twenty-four members throughout the broader region. (Timor-Leste's Provedoria de Direitos Humanos e Justiça, PDHJ, is a member, though not yet a part of ASEAN and therefore AICHR, nor yet fully compliant with the Paris Principles.) As Paris-accredited NHRIs, those of the Philippines, Indonesia, Malaysia and Thailand are full members of the APF; Myanmar and Timor-Leste joined them in participating in the Southeast Asia National Human Rights Institutions Forum (SEANF) (Duxbury and Tan 2019). This forum, in turn, has played an important role within ASEAN human rights processes as an ASEAN partner, and has played a role in standard setting and monitoring (Croydon 2013, 31; Renshaw 2012).

Unlike ASEAN, the Asia Pacific Forum is itself a human rights organisation. As such, its goals and objectives, organisation, development and growth have been oriented towards ensuring accountability for meeting human rights standards. Its Advisory Council of Jurists (ACJ) regularly produces reports on regional human rights issues; one such report in 2010 was dedicated to Sexual Orientation and Gender Identity (ACJ Asia Pacific Forum 2010; Croydon 2013). This report, in turn, emerged in response to an NHRI workshop focused on the Yogyakarta Principles that the APF had hosted in Indonesia. The ACJ reported on each member state's human rights conduct with respect to sexual orientation and gender identity, against five terms of reference: criminal law, anti-discrimination law, recognition of changes of gender, adverse impacts from other laws and the general adequacy of state laws to protect individuals and organisations.

In the years immediately following that report, in what was then perceived to be an 'environment of change and progression' across the region (APF 2013, 8), NHRIs participated in programmes such as the UNDP's 'Being LGBTI in

Asia', and pursued a number of significant initiatives in their own jurisdictions. In the Philippines, for example, the CHRP designated SOGIE and HIV high-priority areas, and in Cebu City the Commission's support encouraged the trans community to lodge hate crime complaints. In Indonesia, KOMNAS HAM became *amicus curiae* in the case of a transgender man who was charged with various offences associated for marrying a woman. The NHRI asserted, 'that the state was not authorised to regulate a person's gender'; the charges were cleared at trial. The oath of office for the Provedor for Human Rights and Justice in Timor-Leste includes a reference to sexual orientation, and the Provedor has followed up on that angle with community engagement (APF 2013, 8–9).

By the mid-2010s, NHRIs were playing significant roles in supporting LGBTIQ communities and both directly and indirectly facilitating their political participation in national-level rights deliberations. This can be clearly observed in a 2015 report of a workshop in Bangkok on the role of NHRIs. The report has a significant number of references to the NHRIs in Southeast Asia, and the various activities, strategies, opportunities and challenges associated with their roles. It lists concrete examples of direct assistance from NHRIs to community members (such as those above), and outlines broader strategic opportunities and collaborative possibilities. These include the role that NHRIs can play *as institutions* in national and regional discussions about agenda setting to include LGBTI issues, especially though HIV/AIDS and health mechanisms and partnerships, and through complaints handling, policy advocacy, education, capacity building and research. While the report is clear about the challenges facing rights advocacy, its advice nonetheless conveys a palpable sense of opportunity, achievement and optimism (UNDP, APF, and APCOM 2015).

Since the mid-2010s, however, the level of openness of the national environment for SOGIESC advocacy has deteriorated substantially in states with full NHRIs. In Malaysia and Indonesia, in particular, as we have seen, this decline is specific to SOGIESC issues; in Thailand and the Philippines, it relates more to the general political context. SOGIESC rights advocate Henry Koh, in a recent analysis of Malaysia's NHRI, SUHAKAM, suggests the continuing importance of these institutions, notwithstanding restrictions they may experience due to curtailed opportunities for political participation. Koh's analysis shows the advantage of institutional status, the role that NHRIs have in socialising recognised international standards and the possibilities the combination of these two elements afford, given judicious leadership. SUHAKAM has engaged in various monitoring programmes of Malaysian institutions for these reasons. A key recent example is SUHAKAM advocacy around the right to health in prisons, and specifically the need to take this right seriously for transgender people, which led to significant interventions in the national debate. Koh argues,

'SUHAKAM has an indispensable role to play in promoting SOGIESC rights in Malaysia and regionally. As an authority mandated to promote and protect all human rights and identify specific groups at risk of human rights violations, SUHAKAM should continue to include LGBTI persons as a priority group to monitor' (Koh 2020, 254).

The Indonesian NHRI, Komnas HAM, engages in mainstreaming practices for LGBTIQ rights under the cover of 'minority rights', which also includes minority religion, race, ethnicity and disability rights. The politicisation of LGBT issues means that support must be guarded; Komnas HAM cannot overtly advocate for them in its programming, publicity or budget processes. The hostile environment also produces increased incidence of stigma, discrimination and violence, making the need for this work more urgent. Komnas HAM has made good use of its formal relationship with the police to manage this challenge, including minority rights training – which it also provides to local governments and civil society. It has made extensive use of the Yogyakarta Principles in such trainings and has distributed them to government departments (health, education, etc.) as a tool in mainstreaming SOGIESC rights. The NHRI utilises the local provenance of the Principles to good effect as a kind of subterfuge, although the need to resort to such moves underlines the broader problem (Komnas HAM 2021).

As these cases indicate, the continuing challenge for Southeast Asian NHRIs will be their willingness, against adverse trends, to retain a full commitment to their investigative and protection mandates, particularly on behalf of those populations most at risk on the basis of their social, political and economic marginalisation (cf. Renshaw, Byrnes, and Durbach 2010).

More broadly, the engagement of national, regional and international level human rights institutions and organisations with the SOGIESC movement across Southeast Asia – whether in full support, or in more contested modes – illustrates a remarkable transformation in the politics and institutional development of human rights across the region. While, clearly, not all formal institutions are on board with including SOGIESC rights in a rights protection agenda, it is salient to observe that a decade ago, approximately when the international human rights regime (in the form of the UN's HRC) formally endorsed SOGIESC rights, many of these regional institutions were themselves only nascent. As they have come into being, and as rights regime infrastructure has increased in density and integration, human rights claiming within the region has consolidated into a new mode of political participation, in which SOGIESC rights claiming specifically is a clear element. I turn now to conclude this Element by recapitulating my broader argument to this effect.

5 SOGIESC, Rights and Political Participation

Rights language has become a prominent discourse for the discussion of sexuality and gender diversity across Southeast Asia. In this Element, I have argued that rights claiming can be understood as a distinctive mode of political participation, with SOGIESC rights claiming – especially for this region – a *newly* available iteration of the wider practice. It is a striking development, emerging alongside ASEAN's new human rights regime, and the broader global application of human rights frames to SOGIESC matters. Advocates and activists across the region have incorporated rights claiming into their activities, through domestic, regional and international rights-based strategies, organisations and institutions. They have used this mode to address forms of societal conflict over sexuality and gender diversity within the region. Social and political responses have been varied. As we have seen from our cases and review of regional organising, there is no consistent set of outcomes for sexuality and gender politics across Southeast Asia. Moral panics in Indonesia and Malaysia are accompanied by moves towards relationship recognition in Thailand and Vietnam. Anti-discrimination legislation is implemented in Thailand and in local government regions in the Philippines, while Singapore refuses to decriminalise male homosexuality – but is happy to welcome those queer workers who can facilitate its economic ambitions. Rather than a consistent set of outcomes, one might see a nascent divergence, with the deterioration in Malaysia and Indonesia appearing set to continue if political trends are sustained, while gains in our other cases seem more secure.

While SOGIESC rights activists were becoming increasingly organised and networked across the region, and linked with international allies, we saw that ASEAN itself implemented a regional human rights regime. From rejecting human rights and democracy in the name of 'Asian values', the region's political elites now turned to human rights as a part of their regional integration project, promising a more 'people-oriented' and 'people-centred' ASEAN. Through this move, the political authorities of the region authorised rights claiming as a legitimate mode of political participation. Rights language was centred within ASEAN rhetoric and incorporated within some existing institutions. New rights-based institutions emerged, headlined by the AICHR and the AHRD.

As we noted, ASEAN's rights turn is commonly criticised for being rhetorical rather than substantive, falling short of world best practice in institutional form, hypocritical in political execution, a fig leaf or bait and switch as far as contentious politics goes in the region (Langlois 2021). While these criticisms, all of which have merit, might be used to dismiss the new rights regime, such a response seems too easy and fails to address why and how political elites allowed a human rights regime to come into being at all. Considering the regime through the opportunities and limitations of its participation in rights praxis provides a more complex analytical reading and is better than shrugging it off into the unfathomable depths of 'the ASEAN way'.

The coincidence of rights regime building in ASEAN with the increased institutionalisation of SOGIESC rights globally complicates the assimilation of rights into ASEAN's regional 'community building' process, and the politics of rights institutionalisation at the state level. Whereas, during the heyday of Asian values, gay rights could be (and routinely were) presumed to be Western imports – because of their articulation *as rights* as much as for any substantive 'gay' reference – once regional states admitted *rights* themselves as legitimate tools for political engagement, the game changed. Rights *to what* became the key question, and the use of institutional power, law, tradition, religion and morality to delineate and contain a substantive rights agenda became significantly more transparent, and more obviously a site of social conflict and competition. Authorities' responses to and management of these rights claims also reveal much about struggles for power and influence, the nature of social conflict, and the intersection of political, economic and ideological interests.

Despite what might appear as an attempt by ASEAN to co-opt rights politics by establishing its own regime, the effort does nonetheless empower rights advocates, not least by providing institutional sanction for engagement, and, hence, openings for critique and counterargument. At the same time, precisely because the satisfaction of rights claims depends on governmental action, the corralling of rights in order to manage populations becomes another way local, state and regional political elites exercise power. Rather than simply refusing rights claims, authorities can shape, mould and instrumentalise them. While rights advocates cannot prevent such efforts, they can politically engage and monitor them, taking the normative content of the international rights regime as a key referent for critique. It was fortuitous, then, that SOGIESC rights come to prominence in Southeast Asia just at the time when SOGIESC advocates' long-standing efforts at rights-based institutional development *beyond* the region, in the international regime, bore fruit. The timing means that efforts to instrumentalise or deflect within Southeast Asia are more obvious and contestable.

I have argued that understanding SOGIESC rights claiming across the region as a mode of political participation enables us to better understand its spread, uptake and impact – but I have also suggested that SOGIESC rights claiming illumines how distinctive a mode rights claiming itself is. As we saw, modes of participation analysis provides an assessment of 'the relationship between institutions and the management, amelioration or containment of conflict', where conflict 'refers to the struggle for access to and the distribution of political resources, authority, and legitimacy' (Jayasuriya and Rodan 2007, 775). The analysis is not just focused on the nature of political institutions, such as new human rights institutions, themselves. Rather, the interest lies in the relationship *between* those institutions and how conflict is organised and structured more broadly within society. What relationships, for example, allowed ASEAN's distinctive human rights regime to emerge, and how do they structure and shape its capacity to have purchase on regional politics? Extending this inquiry to SOGIESC rights claiming: what relationships allow for, prevent, or otherwise shape the use of rights claiming to manage societal conflict over sexuality and gender diversity? This approach illustrates the importance of this new articulation of SOGIESC matters through rights claims, their uptake into (or exclusion from) aligned institutions and the consequences for how social conflict around SOGIESC interacts with rights claiming broadly – its institutional forms and its normative agenda.

In our examination of national cases and regional organising, we have seen queer communities use rights-based strategies as forms of context-specific engagement with political authorities. In some cases, these strategies have been about extending minimal basic protections to recognise and encompass sexuality and gender concerns – for example in relation to HIV/AIDS or health and employment discrimination. In other cases, activists seemed to speak to the void, but over time, their claims have gained measures of traction and even formal support – think of discrimination protection or relationship regulation debates in Thailand and the Philippines. In Singapore, we see continued pragmatic resistance using the law, but also an increased (if still tentative) preparedness to risk protest. In Malaysia and Indonesia, where queer spaces are under renewed threat, we saw that rights institutions (such as NHRIs) can still have impact using general rights claims: protections that apply to all people *also* apply to queer people! This capacity points us to what is distinctive about rights claiming as a mode of political participation.

In each of these quite different contexts of social conflict, existing rights institutions and normative rights claims connect to broader norms and practices at different scales. These connections lend efficacy in the local context, giving rights claims broad normative authority, and are an essential part of the relationship that modes of political participation analysis tracks between institutions and the management of social conflict. As I argued, however, what distinguishes rights claiming is the necessary interaction between its diverse elements: grassroots community support and activism, international norms, protections within state and regional legal systems, engaging international solidarity through civil society and intergovernmental rights mechanisms. Rights are individual *and* collective, national *and* international, in their underlying ideological and institutional structures. These elements, *in concert*, constitute the mode of political participation, interacting across different sites and scales. And it is this interaction that gives rights claiming a strategic and potentially radical power, a power that outweighs the leverage those involved in local rights claiming might ordinarily be thought to have, given their often-marginalised social status.

As activists and advocates have taken up the language and mechanisms of rights claiming to address the social conflicts faced by sexuality and gender diverse communities, new possibilities, political projects and emancipatory visions have been generated. Individuals, communities and organisations have joined together, locally and across the region, to seek recognition of and protection for SOGIESC rights. While much has been achieved, the fight for full realisation of such rights has only just begun, and in many places meets stiff opposition. It has been the central argument of this work that by analysing this SOGIESC rights claiming movement as a newly available mode of political participation, we can come to a clearer understanding of both the bourgeoning of this advocacy activity, and the resultant inconsistent advance of SOGIESC rights in the contemporary Southeast Asian political and social context.

References

Aban, Ananeza, and Jose Monfred C.Sy. 2020. 'Queering Solidarity: Civil Society at the Fringes of ASEAN Regionalism and Alternatives for the LGBTQ+'. *UP CIDS Discussion Paper 2020–11*.

Abdul, Zaina. 2018. 'Being LGBTQ in Brunei'. *New Naratif*, 30 July. https://newnaratif.com/journalism/being-lgbtq-in-brunei/.

ABS-CBN News. (2019). 'Yes or No? Congress Asks Pinoys' Same-Sex Union Stand'. https://news.abs-cbn.com/news/05/22/19/yes-or-no-congress-asks-pinoys-same-sex-union-stand

2020. 'SC Junks Same-Sex Marriage Petition "with Finality"'. https://news.abs-cbn.com/news/01/06/20/sc-junks-same-sex-marriage-petition-with-finality

ACJ Asia Pacific Forum. 2010. 'Human Rights, Sexual Orientation and Gender Identity'. Bali Indonesia: 15th Annual Meeting of the Asia Pacific Forum of National Human Rights Institutions. 3–5 August. www.asiapacificforum.net/resources/acj-report-sogi/.

ACSC/APF. 2011. 'Statement of the 2011 ASEAN Civil Society Conference/ASEAN Peoples' Forum'. 3–5 May. http://nsinitiative.net/wp-content/uploads/2019/10/2011-ACSC-APF-2011-Statement.pdf.

Afifi, Numan. 2021. Interview with Numan Afifi – Pelangi Campaign.

Al-Mohdhar, Mayang, and Sarah Ngu. 2019. 'History Shows Gender, Sexual Diversity Not Alien to Malaysia'. *Europe Solidaire Sans Frontières*, 1 July. www.europe-solidaire.org/spip.php?article49802.

APCOM. 2016. Engagement of LGBTI Activists in the UPR to Promote, Protect and Advance SOGIE Rights. https://youtu.be/lIZasyEIAoc.

2017. 'The Khmer LGBTIQ+ Experience'. December 4–8. https://apcom.org/wp-content/uploads/2018/01/The-Khmer-LBGTIQ-experience-Revised-1.pdf.

2020. 'Six Asian Countries Remind UNAIDS Executive Director to Not Forget the Region's Key Population Needs for World AIDS Day 2020'. 30 November. www.apcom.org/six-asian-countries-remind-unaids-executive-director-to-not-forget-the-regions-key-population-needs-for-world-aids-day-2020/.

NHRCB (National Human Rights Commission of Bangladesh). 2013. 'Report to the Regional National Human Rights Institutions Project on Inclusion, the Right to Health and Sexual Orientation and Gender Identity'. APF, UNDP, IDLO. 11 October 2012. www.idlo.int/publications/regional-report-capacity-national-human-rights-institutions-address-human-rights.

ARC International, ILGA World, and ISHR. 2019. '#RenewIESOGI'. http://arc-international.net/wp-content/uploads/RenewIESOGI_report.pdf.

ASC. 2012. 'The 2012 LGBTIQ Caucus Statement'. http://herlounge.blogspot.com.au/2012/12/phnom-penh-cambodia.html.

———. 2013. 'Press Release: ASEAN SOGIE Caucus Launches Regional Campaign Criticizing Declarations on Women and Children'. 15 October. www.facebook.com/notes/asean-sogie-caucus/press-release-asean-sogie-caucus-launches-regional-campaign-criticizing-declarat/537979016294029.

———. 2015. Queering ASEAN Integration. www.youtube.com/watch?v=47C_kQfOo5g.

———. 2017. 'Joint Submission of the Civil Society Organisations on the Situation of Lesbian, Gay, Bisexual, Transgender, Intersex and Queer Persons in the Philippines'. https://aseansogiecaucus.org/images/resources/upr-reports/Philippines/Philippines-UPR-JointReport-3rdCycle.pdf.

———. 2018. 'The Rainbow in Context – LGBTIQ Persons in Southeast Asia'. https://aseansogiecaucus.org/images/resources/publications/The%20Rainbow%20in%20Context%20-%20LGBTIQ%20Persons%20in%20SEA.pdf

———. 2019. 'Regional Groups Urged AICHR to Address Human Rights Concerns Arising from Brunei's Syariah Penal Code'. 12 April. https://aseansogiecaucus.org/statements/asc-statements/133-regional-groups-urged-aichr-to-address-human-rights-concerns-arising-from-brunei-s-syariah-penal-code.

———. 2021a. 'Be/Longings: Southeast Asia Queer Cultural Festival 2021'. https://seaqcf.net/program/featured-works.

———. 2021b. Rainbow Parl 2021: Status of LGBTIQ and Legislation in Southeast Asia. www.youtube.com/watch?v=qiXIorcDscI&t=39s.

———. 2021c. 'Southeast Asian Queer Cultural Festival'. 13 February–13 March. https://seaqcf.net/.

ASEAN Secretariat. 2015. 'ASEAN 2025 Forging Ahead Together', December. www.asean.org/storage/2016/01/ASEAN-2025-Forging-Ahead-Together-2nd-Reprint-Dec-2015.pdf.

BBC News, 2016. 'The Sudden Intensity of Indonesia's Anti-Gay Onslaught'. www.bbc.com/news/world-asia-35657114.

Beltran, Michael. 2020. 'Philippine LGBT Activists Fight Duterte's Machismo with Solidarity'. *The News Lens International Edition*. https://international.thenewslens.com/article/137151.

Bernal, Buena. 2015. 'SC Asked: Allow Same-Sex Marriage in PH'. *Rappler*, 25 May. www.rappler.com/nation/same-sex-marriage-petition-supreme-court.

Bexley, Angie, and Sharon Bessell. 2020. 'Legislating Self-Reliance and Family Values in the Time of Coronavirus?' *New Mandala* (blog), 9 September. www.newmandala.org/legislating-self-reliance-and-family-values-in-the-time-of-coronavirus/.

Black, Ann. 2019. 'Casting the First Stone: The Significance of Brunei Darussalam's Syariah Penal Code Order for LGBT Bruneians'. *Australian Journal of Asian Law* 20 (1): 1–17.

Blackwood, Evelyn. 2010. *Falling into the Lesbi World: Desire and Difference in Indonesia*. Honolulu: University of Hawai'i Press.

——— 2012. '"Lesbians", Modernity and Global Translation: Female Sexualities in Indonesia'. In *Routledge Handbook of Sexuality, Health and Rights*, edited by Peter Aggleton and Richard G. Parker, 69–76. London: Routledge.

Boellstorff, Tom. 2007. *A Coincidence of Desires: Anthropology, Queer Studies, Indonesia*. Durham: Duke University Press.

——— 2016. 'Against State Straightism: Five Principles for Including LGBT Indonesians'. *E-International Relations* (blog), 21 March. www.e-ir.info/2016/03/21/against-state-straightism-five-principles-for-including-lgbt-indonesians/.

——— 2020. 'Om Toleran Om: Four Indonesian Reflections on Digital Heterosexism'. *Media, Culture & Society* 42 (1): 7–24. https://doi.org/10.1177/0163443719884066.

Boonlert, Thana. 2020. 'Gender Recognition Bill Set to Be Tabled'. *Bangkok Post*, 6 August. www.bangkokpost.com/thailand/general/1963599/gender-recognition-bill-set-to-be-tabled.

Bosia, Michael, Sandra M. McEvoy, and Momin Rahman, eds. 2019. *The Oxford Handbook of Global LGBT and Sexual Diversity Politics*. Oxford: Oxford University Press. https://doi.org/10.1093/oxfordhb/9780190673741.013.11.

Brown, David. 2010. 'Making Room for Sexual Orientation and Gender Identity in International Human Rights Law: An Introduction to the Yogyakarta Principles'. *Michigan Journal of International Law* 31 (Summer): 821–79.

Calera, Lex. 2019. 'Multiple Cases of Trans Discrimination Motivate Passionate Campaign for Gender Equality in the Philippines'. *Vice*, 14 August. www.vice.com/en/article/gyzbpq/multiple-cases-of-trans-discrimination-motivate-passionate-campaign-for-gender-equality-in-the-philippines.

Cardozo, Bradley. 2014. 'A "Coming Out" Party in Congress? LGBT Advocacy and Party-List Politics in the Philippines'. Master's Thesis, UCLA. https://escholarship.org/uc/item/49v8j2wx.

Carroll, Toby, Shahar Hameiri, and Lee Jones, eds. 2020. *The Political Economy of Southeast Asia: Politics and Uneven Development under Hyperglobalisation*. Switzerland: Palgrave MacMillan.

Castañeda, Jan. 2020. Interview with Jan Castañeda – ASEAN SOGIE Caucus.

Chan, Sek Keong. 2019. 'Equal Justice under the Constitution and Section 377A of the Penal Code: The Road Not Taken'. *Singapore Academy of Law Journal* 31 (2) : 773–844.

Chase. 2017. 'Anti-Discrimination Ordinances Across the Philippines'. *Transgender Philippines* (blog), 15 May. www.transph.org/information/ philippine-anti-discrimination-ordinances/.

Cho, Jasmine. 2019. 'What Happened to Harapan's Vow to Improve Human Rights?' *Malaysiakini*, 11 December. www.malaysiakini.com/news/ 503280.

Chong, Jean. 2020. Interview with Jean Chong – Sayoni.

Chua, Lynette J. 2014. *Mobilizing Gay Singapore: Rights and Resistance in an Authoritarian State*. Pennsylvania: Temple University Press.

2022. *Politics of Rights and Southeast Asia*. Cambridge: Cambridge University Press.

CNA. 2020. 'Thai Cabinet Backs Bill Allowing Same-Sex Unions'. 8 July. www.channelnewsasia.com/news/asia/thailand-cabinet-backs-bill-allowing-same-sex-unions-12914716.

Coconuts Jakarta. 2016. 'Senior Minister Luhut Panjaitan: Members of LGBT Community Have Rights and Must Be Protected'. 12 February. https:// coconuts.co/jakarta/lifestyle/senior-minister-luhut-panjaitan-members-lgbt-community-have-rights-and-must-be-protected/.

Coconuts Manila. 2019. 'LGBT Group Speaks Out against PH Congress' Online Poll on Same-Sex Unions'. 22 May. https://coconuts.co/manila/ news/lgbt-group-speaks-out-against-ph-congress-online-poll-on-same-sex-unions/.

Coleman, Eli, Mariette Pathy Allen, and Jessie V. Ford. 2018. 'Gender Variance and Sexual Orientation Among Male Spirit Mediums in Myanmar'. *Archives of Sexual Behavior* 47 (4): 987–98. https://doi.org/10.1007/ s10508-018-1172-0.

Cook, Erin. 2019. 'Will Duterte Help Win the Battle for Gay Rights in the Philippines?' *The Diplomat*, 16 August. https://thediplomat.com/2019/08/ will-duterte-help-win-the-battle-for-gay-rights-in-the-philippines/.

Cristobal, Ging. 2020. Interview with Ging Cristobal – OutRight Action International.

Croydon, Silvia. 2013. 'Two Rights Paths: East Asia's Emerging Regional Human Rights Framework'. *Asia Pacific Perspectives* 11 (1): 22–35.

Davies, Mathew. 2021. 'How Regional Organizations Respond to Human Rights: ASEAN's Ritualism in Comparative Perspective'. *Journal of Human Rights* 20 (2): 245–62. https://doi.org/10.1080/14754835 .2020.1841607.

Davies, Sharyn. 2020. 'What's Driving Indonesia's Moral Turn?' *New Mandala* (blog), 25 May. www.newmandala.org/whats-driving-indonesias-moral-turn/.

Destination Justice. 2017. 'LGBTIQ Rights in Southeast Asia: Implementing Recommendations from the Universal Periodic Review'. In *The Universal Periodic Review of Southeast Asia: Civil Society Perspectives*, edited by James Gomez and Robin Ramcharan, 97–111. New York: Springer.

——— 2018. 'Revealing the Rainbow: The Human Rights Situation of Southeast Asia's LGBTIQ Communities and Their Defenders. https://aseansogiecau cus.org/resources/publications.

Deutsche Welle. 2018. 'Indonesia Debates Bill Criminalizing Gay Sex and Any Sex Outside of Marriage'. 6 February. www.dw.com/en/indonesia-debates-bill-criminalizing-gay-sex-and-any-sex-outside-of-marriage/a-424672 20.

Duggan, Lisa. 2002. 'The New Homonormativity: The Sexual Politics of Neoliberalism'. In *Materializing Democracy: Toward a Revitalized Cultural Politics*, edited by Russ Castronovo and Dana D. Nelson, 175–94, Durham and London: Dule University Press.

Duxbury, Alison, and Hsien-Li Tan. 2019. *Can ASEAN Take Human Rights Seriously?* Integration through Law: The Role of Law and the Rule of Law in ASEAN Integration. Cambridge: Cambridge University Press. https://doi.org/10.1017/9781108566414.

Ewing, Michael. 2020. 'The Use of the Term LGBT in Indonesia and Its Real-World Consequences'. *Melbourne Asia Review*, no. 2 (May). https://doi .org/10.37839/MAR2652-550X2.11.

Falcis v. *Civil Registrar General, G.R. No. 217910*. 2019. http://sc .judiciary.gov.ph/8227.

FMT. 2021. 'Stop Using LGBT Community as Punching Bag, Says Rights Group'. 20 January. www.freemalaysiatoday.com/category/nation/ 2021/01/20/stop-using-lgbt-community-as-punching-bag-says-rights-group/.

Fonbuena, Carmela. 2018. 'Philippine Lawyer Finds Unlikely Ally in Duterte in Fight to Legalise Gay Marriage'. *The Guardian*, 18 June. www .theguardian.com/world/2018/jun/18/philippines-lawyer-gay-marriage-duterte-church.

Gadong, Early Sol A., ed. 2021. *ASEAN Queer Imaginings*. Quezon City: *ASC*. https://aseansogiecaucus.org/news/asc-news/160-asean-queer-imaginings-collection-of-writings-by-lgbtiq-thinkers.

Gamboa, Lance Calvin L., Emerald Jay D. Ilac, Athena May Jean M. Carangan, and Julia Izah S. Agida. 2020. 'Queering Public Leadership: The Case of Lesbian, Gay, Bisexual and Transgender Leaders in the Philippines'. *Leadership* 17 (2): 191–211. https://doi.org/10.1177/1742715020953273.

Geddie, John. 2020. 'Gay Rights: The Taboo Subject in Singapore's Election'. *Reuters*, 8 July. www.reuters.com/article/us-singapore-election-lgbt-idUSKBN2490GS.

Gerard, Kelly. 2014. *ASEAN's Engagement of Civil Society: Regulating Dissent*. London: Palgrave Macmillan. https://doi.org/10.1057/9781137359476.

Geronimo, Luis Jose F. 2020. 'Rising Above Contempt: SOGIESC Equality and LGBTQI+ Rights in Philippine Law through the Lens of Falcis v. Civil Registrar General'. *Ateneo Law Journal* 64 (4): 309–1411.

Gilbert, David. 2013. 'Categorizing Gender in Queer Yangon'. *Journal of Social Issues in Southeast Asia* 28 (2): 241. https://doi.org/10.1355/sj28-2c.

Glauert, Rik. 2019. 'Transgender Activists in Thailand Propose Law to Protect Their Rights'. *Gay Star News*, 28 July. www.gaystarnews.com/article/transgender-activists-in-thailand-propose-law-to-protect-their-rights/.

Gomez, James, and Robin Ramcharan, eds. 2020. *National Human Rights Institutions in Southeast Asia*. Singapore: Palgrave MacMillan.

Gorey, Colm. 2019. '"We're Not like San Francisco": Singapore PM Addresses LGBTQ Rights in City State'. *Silicon Republic*, 27 June. www.siliconrepublic.com/careers/singapore-lgbtq-rights.

Graham Davies, Sharyn. 2016. 'Indonesian "Tolerance" under Strain as Anti-LGBT Furore Grows'. *Asian Studies Association of Australia*, 20 March. http://asaa.asn.au/indonesian-tolerance-under-strain-as-anti-lgbt-furore-grows/.

——— 2018. 'The West Can Learn from Southeast Asia's Transgender Heritage'. *Aeon*, 12 June. https://aeon.co/essays/the-west-can-learn-from-southeast-asias-transgender-heritage.

——— 2019. 'Waria'. In *Global Encyclopedia of Lesbian, Gay, Bisexual, Transgender, and Queer History*, edited by Howard Chiang *et al., 1717–*20. Farmington Hills, Mich: Gale Cengage.

——— 2020. 'Sexual Citizenship Re-Centred: Gender and Sexual Diversity in Indonesia'. In *The SAGE Handbook of Global Sexualities*, edited by

Zowie Davy, Ana Santos, Chiara Bertone, Ryan Thoreson, and Saskia Wieringa, 688–704. London: Sage. https://doi.org/10.4135/9781529714364.n32.

Gross, Aeyal. 2018. 'Homoglobalism: The Emergence of Global Gay Governance'. In *Queering International Law: Possibilities, Alliances, Complications, Risks*, edited by Dianne Otto, 148–70. Abingdon: Routledge.

Han, Kirsten, and Joy Ho. 2020a. 'Growing a Movement in Activism-Averse Singapore'. *New Naratif* (blog), 15 January. https://newnaratif.com/journalism/growing-a-movement-in-activism-averse-singapore/share/pybxr/59e55259f971b935b82107ff58b740ab/.

2020b. 'The Limits of Singaporean Activism?' *New Naratif* (blog), 17 January. https://newnaratif.com/journalism/the-limits-of-singaporean-activism/share/cwguhz/b1e62d03dc50c0655a460c8ef12513cf/.

Hanara, Desi. 2019. *A Decade in Review: Assessing the Performance of the AICHR to Uphold the Protection Mandates.* Forum-Asia. https://www.forum-asia.org/?p=29041

HDT. n.d. 'Singapore: Two Separate Cases before the Court of Appeal'. www.humandignitytrust.org./what-we-do/cases/singapore-two-separate-cases-before-the-court-of-appeal/.

Hefner, Robert W., and Barbara Watson Andaya, eds. 2018. *Routledge Handbook of Contemporary Indonesia*. Abingdon: Routledge.

Herrera, Felix. 2020. 'A Rundown on the History of Same-Sex Marriage in the Philippines'. *Esquire*, 7 January. www.esquiremag.ph/politics/news/same-sex-marriage-in-the-philippines-a2292-20200107.

HRW. 2014. 'I'm Scared to Be a Woman'. 24 September www.hrw.org/report/2014/09/24/im-scared-be-woman/human-rights-abuses-against-transgender-people-malaysia.

2021. 'Malaysia: Government Steps Up Attacks on LGBT People'. 25 January. www.hrw.org/news/2021/01/25/malaysia-government-steps-attacks-lgbt-people.

ILGA. 2017. UPR Outcome of the Philippines | HRC 36. www.youtube.com/watch?v=bcpDdU3m24 g.

Jackson, Peter A. 2003. 'Performative Genders, Perverse Desires: A Bio-History of Thailand's Same-Sex and Transgender Cultures'. *Intersections: Gender and Sexuality in Asia and the Pacific*, no. 9 (August). http://intersections.anu.edu.au/issue9_contents.html.

2013. 'Cultural Pluralism and Sex/Gender Diversity in Thailand: Introduction'. In *Phet Lak Chet-Si: Phahuwattanatham Thang-Phet Nai Sangkhom Thai – Cultural Pluralism and Sex/Gender Diversity in*

Thailand, edited by Narupon Duangwesis, 14–17. Bangkok: Princess Sirindhorn Anthropology Centre.

2001. 'Pre-Gay, Post-Queer: Thai Perspectives on Proliferating Gender/Sex Diversity in Asia'. *Journal of Homosexuality* 40 (3–4): 1–25. https://doi .org/10.1300/J082v40n03_01.

2011. *Queer Bangkok Twenty-First-Century Markets, Media, and Rights*. Hong Kong: Hong Kong University Press.

Jackson, Peter A., and Gerard Sullivan, eds. 1999. *Lady Boys, Tom Boys, Rent Boys: Male and Female Homosexualities in Contemporary Thailand*. Birmingham: Harrington Park Press.

Jayasuriya, Kanishka, and Garry Rodan. 2007. 'Beyond Hybrid Regimes: More Participation, Less Contestation in Southeast Asia'. *Democratization* 14 (5): 773–94.

JFS. 2021. 'Proposed Amendments to Further Criminalize LGBTQ Persons by Deputy Minister of Religious Minister are Unconstitutional'. 25 January. https://justiceforsisters.wordpress.com/2021/01/25/proposed-amendments- to-further-criminalize-lgbtq-persons-by-deputy-minister-of-religious- minister-are-unconstitutional/.

Jocson, Ellisiah Uy, and Wisnu Adihartono. 2020. 'A Comparative Analysis of the Status of Homosexual Men in Indonesia and the Philippines'. *Journal of Southeast Asian Human Rights* 4 (1): 271. https://doi.org/10.19184/ jseahr.v4i1.12810.

Jommaroeng, Rapeepun. 2021. Interview with Rapeepun Jommaroeng – Rainbow Sky Association of Thailand.

Khanis, Suvianita. 2013. 'Human Rights and the LGBTI Movement in Indonesia'. *Asian Journal of Women's Studies* 19 (1): 127–38. https://doi .org/10.1080/12259276.2013.11666145.

Kirby, Michael. 2013. 'The Sodomy Offence: England's Least Lovely Criminal Law Export?' In *Human Rights, Sexual Orientation and Gender Identity in the Commonwealth: Struggles for Decriminalisation and Change*, edited by Corinne Lennox and Matthew Waites, 61–82. London: Human Rights Consortium, Institute of Commonwealth Studies.

Koh, Henry. 2020. 'Bridging Gaps and Hopes: Malaysia's National Human Rights Commission and Rights Related to SOGIESC'. In *National Human Rights Institutions in Southeast Asia*, edited by James Gomez and Robin Ramcharan, 241–59. Singapore: Palgrave MacMillan.

Komnas HAM. 2021. 'Komnas HAM @43 Mins Till1:07'. In *Rainbow Parliament (Day II) Conference Online*, edited by ASC. www .facebook.com/531030516988879/videos/345473789837824.

Kumar, P. Prem. 2019. 'Anwar Faces New Sexual Assault Charge in Power Struggle'. *Nikkei Asian Review*, 6 December. https://asia.nikkei.com/ Politics/Anwar-faces-new-sexual-assault-charge-in-power-struggle.

Kurohi, Rei. 2020. 'High Court Dismisses Challenges against Law That Criminalises Sex between Men'. *The Straits Times*, 30 March. www .straitstimes.com/singapore/high-court-rejects-all-three-challenges-against-section-377a.

Lam, Lydia. 2021. 'All Three Men to Appeal Dismissal of Their Challenges against Section 377A'. *Channel News Asia*, 31 March. www.channelnewsasia.com/ news/singapore/all-three-men-to-appeal-dismissal-of-their-challenges-against-12592934.

Langford, Malcolm, and Cosette D. Creamer. 2017. 'The Toonen Decision: Domestic and International Impact'. *SSRN Electronic Journal*, 36. https:// doi.org/10.2139/ssrn.3063850.

Langlois, Anthony J. 2001. *The Politics of Justice and Human Rights: Southeast Asia and Universalist Theory*. Cambridge: Cambridge University Press.

2014. 'Human Rights, "Orientation," and ASEAN'. *Journal of Human Rights* 13 (3): 307–21. https://doi.org/10.1080/14754835.2014.919215.

2019. 'Making LGBT Rights into Human Rights'. In *The Oxford Handbook of Global LGBT and Sexual Diversity Politics*, edited by Michael Bosia, Sandra M. McEvoy, and Momin Rahman, 75–88. Oxford: Oxford University Press. https://doi.org/10.1093/oxfordhb/9780190673741.013.21.

2021. 'Human Rights in Southeast Asia: ASEAN's Rights Regime after Its First Decade'. *Journal of Human Rights* 20 (2): 151–57. https://doi.org/10 .1080/14754835.2020.1843144.

Langlois, Anthony J., and Mathew Davies, eds. 2021. *'ASEAN and Human Rights Governance' Special Issue Journal of Human Rights 20:2*. New York: Taylor & Francis.

Langlois, Anthony J., Cai Wilkinson, Paula Gerber, and Baden Offord. 2017. 'Community, Identity, Orientation: Sexuality, Gender and Rights in ASEAN'. *The Pacific Review* 30 (5): 710–28. https://doi.org/10.1080/ 09512748.2017.1294613.

Lawson, Stephanie. 1999. 'Perspectives on the Study of Culture and International Politics: From Nihonjinron to the New Asianism'. *Asia-Pacific Review* 6 (2): 24–41. https://doi.org/10.1080/13439009908720015.

Lennox, Corinne, and Matthew Waites. 2013. *Human Rights, Sexual Orientation and Gender Identity in the Commonwealth: Struggles for Decriminalisation and Change*. London: Human Rights Consortium, Institute of Commonwealth Studies.

Liang, Jamison. 2010. 'Homophobia on the Rise'. *Inside Indonesia*, 14 June. www.insideindonesia.org/homophobia-on-the-rise.

Listiorini, Dina. 2020. 'Online Hate Speech'. *Inside Indonesia*, no. 139 (January). www.insideindonesia.org/online-hate-speech.

Llewellyn, Aisyah. 2018. 'Punitive Measures: Indonesia's New Draft Criminal Code'. *Lowy Institute*, 9 February. www.lowyinstitute.org/the-interpreter/punitive-measures-indonesias-new-draft-criminal-code.

Lum, Selina. 2021. 'Challenge against Section 377A: Chief Justice Says Govt's "Compromise" on Enforcement Should Be Considered'. *The Straits Times*, 25 January. www.straitstimes.com/singapore/courts-crime/challenge-against-section-377a-chief-justice-says-govts-compromise-on.

Mahavongtrakul, Melalin. 2019. 'The Right to Title Change'. *Bangkok Post*, 29 July. www.bangkokpost.com/life/social-and-lifestyle/1720675/the-right-to-title-change.

Mendez, Christina. 2019. 'Duterte Favors Anti-Discrimination Law over SOGIE'. *Philstar.com*, 12 September. www.philstar.com/headlines/2019/09/12/1951158/duterte-favors-anti-discrimination-law-over-sogie.

Mirtha, Shenntyara. 2017. 'Thailand Proposed Law to Allow Gender Certification'. *The ASEAN Post*, 26 July. https://theaseanpost.com/article/thailand-proposed-law-allow-gender-certification.

Morgan, Joe. 2019. 'Gay High School Law Student Shot Dead for Trying to Do Human Rights Work'. *Gay Star News*, 15 June. www.gaystarnews.com/article/gay-high-school-law-student-shot-dead-for-trying-to-do-human-rights-work/.

Muna-McQuay, Lazeena. 2017. 'Gender Law Ignored as Inequality Persists'. *Bangkok Post*, 9 March. www.bangkokpost.com/opinion/opinion/1211381/gender-law-ignored-as-inequality-persists.

Muntarbhorn, Vitit. 2018. 'Challenges to Gender Equality in Thailand'. *Bangkok Post*, 8 March. www.bangkokpost.com/opinion/opinion/1424306/challenges-to-gender-equality-in-thailand.

2021. Interview with Vitit Muntarbhorn – Inaugural UN SOGI Independent Expert.

Nguyen, Yen. 2020. Interview with Yen Nguyen – ASEAN SOGIE Caucus.

Nonato, Vince. 2020. 'Groups Call Duterte's Pardon of Pemberton a "Direct Attack" on Trans People'. *Rappler*, 9 September. www.rappler.com/moveph/groups-call-duterte-pardon-pemberton-direct-attack-trans-people.

Nufael, Ali. 2018. 'Malaysian Religious Affairs Minister Voices Support for LGBT Workers'. *BenarNews*, 17 July. www.benarnews.org/english/news/malaysian/Malaysia-rights-07172018163623.html.

Oetomo, Dédé. 2013. 'New Kids on the Block: Human Rights, Sexual Orientation, and Gender Identity in Southeast Asia'. *Asian-Pacific Law & Policy Journal* 14 (2): 118–31.

Offord, Baden. 2003. *Homosexual Rights as Human Rights: Activism in Indonesia, Singapore and Australia*. Oxford: Peter Lang.

O'Flaherty, Michael. 2015. 'The Yogyakarta Principles at Ten'. *Nordic Journal of Human Rights* 33 (4): 280–98. https://doi.org/10.1080/18918131.2015.1127009.

Ong, Aihwa, and Michael Peletz, eds. 1995. *Bewitching Women, Pious Men: Gender and Body Politics in Southeast Asia*. Berkeley: University of California Press.

Oogachaga and Pink Dot. 2016. 'Joint Submission Stake-Holder Report UPR 24'. Joint Submission. Geneva: United Nations. https://ilga.org/downloads/Singapore_STAKEHOLDERS_REPORT.pdf.

Palo, Jed. 2020. 'LGBTQI+ Filipinos Still Belittled, Silenced under Duterte'. *UPLB Perspective*, 12 September. https://uplbperspective.org/2020/09/12/lgbtqi-filipinos-still-belittled-silenced-under-duterte/.

Pang Khee Teik. 2019. 'How Selective Liberal Outrage against Brunei is Missing the Point'. *Queer Lapis* (blog), 5 April. www.queerlapis.com/how-selective-liberal-outrage-against-brunei-is-missing-the-point/.

2021. Interview with Pang Khee Teik – Seksualiti Merdeka.

Panti, Llanesca. 2020. 'Military Opposes SOGIE Bill, Says It Could Compromise Rights of Majority'. *GMA News Online*, 28 August. www.gmanetwork.com/news/news/nation/753302/military-opposes-sogie-bill-says-it-could-compromise-rights-of-majority/story/.

Paramaditha, Intan. 2016. 'The LGBT Debate and the Fear of "Gerakan"'. *The Jakarta Post*, 27 February. www.thejakartapost.com/news/2016/02/27/the-lgbt-debate-and-the-fear-gerakan.html.

Partogi, Sebastian. 2021. 'LGBT People Hope to Gain Sense of Safety, Belonging'. *The Jakarta Post*, 19 January. www.thejakartapost.com/life/2021/01/18/lgbt-people-hope-to-gain-sense-of-safety-belonging.html.

Pascual, Patrick King. 2012. 'Ladlad: Nine Years of Fighting for LGBT Rights'. *Outrage*, 17 September. https://outragemag.com/ladlad-partylist-nine-years-of-fighting-for-lgbt-rights/.

Pelangi Campaign. 2018. 'PELANGI Campaign on Twitter'. *Twitter*, 20 August. https://twitter.com/pelangicampaign/status/1031398190270963712.

Peletz, Michael G. 1988. *A Share of the Harvest: Kinship, Property, and Social History Among the Malays of Rembau*. Berkeley: University of California Press.

1996. *Reason and Passion: Representations of Gender in a Malay Society.* Berkeley: University of California Press.

2009. *Gender Pluralism: Southeast Asia since Early Modern Times.* New York: Routledge.

Petkovic, Josko. 1999a. 'Dédé Oetomo Talks on Reyog Ponorogo'. *Intersections: Gender and Sexuality in Asia and the Pacific*, no. 2 (May). http://intersections.anu.edu.au/issue2_contents.html.

1999b. 'Waiting for Karila: Bending Time, Theory and Gender in Java and Bali (With Reflections for a Documentary Treatment)'. *Intersections: Gender and Sexuality in Asia and the Pacific*, no. 2 (May). http://intersections.anu.edu.au/issue2_contents.html.

Pham, Khanhbinh (Eric). 2020. Interview with Eric Pham – Hanoi Queer.

Pisey, Ly, Chey Leaphy Heng, and Sally Low. 2019. 'Advocating for the Rainbow Family in Cambodia'. *Australian Journal of Asian Law* 20 (1): 13.

Platt, Maria, Sharyn Graham Davies, and Linda Rae Bennett. 2018. 'Contestations of Gender, Sexuality and Morality in Contemporary Indonesia'. *Asian Studies Review* 42 (1): 1–15. https://doi.org/10.1080/10357823.2017.1409698.

Poonkasetwattana, Midnight. 2021. Interview with Midnight Poonkasetwattana – APCOM.

Poushter, Jacob, and Nicholas O. Kent. 2020. 'The Global Divide on Homosexuality Persists'. *Pew Research Center.* 25 June 2020. https://www.pewresearch.org/global/2020/06/25/global-divide-on-homosexuality-persists/

Prachatai. 2019a. 'Being LGBT in Thailand: Transgender Student Files Complaint with Gender Discrimination Committee on Uniform Case'. *Europe Solidaire Sans Frontières*, 22 January. www.europe-solidaire.org/spip.php?article47678.

2019b. 'Victory for Trans Students at Chulalongkorn University'. 13 November. https://prachatai.com/english/node/8274.

Promchertchoo, Pichayada. 2020. 'Thailand's Civil Partnership Bill Sparks Further Debate on Same-Sex Couple Rights'. *Channel News Asia*, 27 July. www.channelnewsasia.com/news/asia/thailand-civil-partnership-lgbtiq-gender-equality-discrimination-12954614.

Puar, Jasbir K. 2007. *Terrorist Assemblages: Homonationalism in Queer Times.* Durham: Duke University Press.

Queer Lapis. 2020. 'Stop Intimidating Human Rights Defenders Who Question LGBTQ-Related Government Policies'. 5 August. www.queerlapis.com/stop-intimidating-human-rights-defenders-who-question-lgbtq-related-government-policies/.

Radics, George Baylon. 2021. 'Challenging Anti-Sodomy Laws in Singapore and the Former British Colonies of ASEAN'. *Journal of Human Rights* 20 (2): 211–27.

Rahman, Momin. 2014. *Homosexualities, Muslim Cultures and Modernity.* Basingstoke: Palgrave Macmillan.

Rao, Rahul. 2020. *Out of Time.* Oxford: Oxford University Press.

Rappler. 2016. 'Minister: I'm Not against LGBT, Just Their Public Displays of Affection'. 26 January. https://rappler.com/world/asia-pacific/lgbt-ban-campus-minister-nasir.

——— 2019. 'What is QC's Ordinance against LGBTQ+ Discrimination All About?' 14 August. www.rappler.com/newsbreak/iq/things-to-know-quezon-city-ordinance-against-lgbtq-discrimination.

Reid, Anthony. 1988. *Southeast Asia in the Age of Commerce, 1450–1680: The Lands below the Winds.* New Haven: Yale University Press.

Renshaw, Catherine, Andrew Byrnes, and Andrea Durbach. 2010. 'Human Rights Protection in the Pacific: The Emerging Role of National Human Rights Institutions in the Region'. *New Zealand Journal of Public and International Law* 8 (1): 117–44.

Renshaw, Catherine Shanahan. 2012. 'National Human Rights Institutions and Civil Society Organizations: New Dynamics of Engagement at Domestic, Regional, and International Levels'. *Global Governance: A Review of Multilateralism and International Organizations* 18 (3): 299–316.

——— 2013. 'The ASEAN Human Rights Declaration 2012'. *Human Rights Law Review* 13 (3): 557–79. https://doi.org/10.1093/hrlr/ngt016.

Reuters. 2017. 'Indonesia Court Rejects Petition to Bar Consensual Sex Outside Marriage'. 14 December. www.reuters.com/article/us-indonesia-court-adultery-idUSKBN1E80BI.

——— 2018. 'Draft Proposals in Indonesian Parliament Aim to Ban Extramarital Sex'.29 January. www.reuters.com/article/us-indonesia-adultery-idUSKBN1FI13X.

Rodan, Garry. 2018. *Participation without Democracy: Containing Conflict in Southeast Asia.* Ithaca: Cornell University Press.

——— 2022. *Civil Society in Southeast Asia: The Struggle for Power.* Cambridge: Cambridge University Press.

Rodan, Garry, and Jacqui Baker. 2020. 'Explaining Political Regimes in Southeast Asia: A Modes of Participation Framework'. In *The Political Economy of Southeast Asia: Politics and Uneven Development under Hyperglobalisation*, edited by Toby Carroll, Shahar Hameiri, and Lee Jones, 87–109. Switzerland: Palgrave MacMillan.

Rodriguez, Diego Garcia. 2019. 'The Muslim Waria of Yogyakarta'. *TSQ: Transgender Studies Quarterly* 6 (3): 368–85. https://doi.org/10.1215/23289252-7549470.

Rodriguez, Diego Garcia, and Khanis Suvianita. 2020. 'How Indonesia's LGBT Community is Making a Difference Amid COVID-19'. *The Conversation*, 26 June. http://theconversation.com/how-indonesias-lgbt-community-is-making-a-difference-amid-covid-19-140063.

Sanders, Douglas. 2019. 'Thailand and "Diverse Sexualities"'. *Australian Journal of Asian Law* 20 (1): 1–21.

2020a. 'Sex and Gender Diversity'. In *Routledge Handbook of Contemporary Thailand*, edited by Pavin Chachavalpongpun, 340–52. New York: Routledge.

2020b. 'Sex and Gender Diversity in Southeast Asia'. *Journal of Southeast Asian Human Rights* 4 (2): 357–405. https://doi.org/10.19184/jseahr.v4i2.17281.

2009. '377 and the Unnatural Afterlife of British Colonialism in Asia'. *Asian Journal of Comparative Law* 4 (1). 1–51. www.degruyter.com/view/j/asjcl.2009.4.1/asjcl.2009.4.1.1176/asjcl.2009.4.1.1176.xml.

Santiago, Charles. 2019. 'Mahathir's Pakatan Harapan Has Mixed Track Record on Changing Human Rights Laws in Malaysia – but Progress Takes Time'. *South China Morning Post*, 9 May. www.scmp.com/week-asia/opinion/article/3009575/mahathirs-pakatan-harapan-has-mixed-track-record-changing-human.

Shine, Robert. 2019. 'Catholic Sister in Philippines Strongly Endorses LGBTQ Non-Discrimination Bill'. *New Ways Ministry*, 10 September. www.newwaysministry.org/2019/09/10/catholic-sister-in-philippines-strongly-endorses-anti-lgbtq-non-discrimination-bill/.

Silverio, Ryan. 2019. 'Brunei: A Reflection on the Ongoing Saga'. *ARROW-AFC: The Right to Sexuality*, 25 (1): 30–31.

2020. Interview with Ryan Silverio – ASEAN SOGIE Caucus.

2021. 'Personal Communication'.

Sim, Dewey. 2020. 'Singapore: Gay Sex Still Illegal, Judge Throws Out Section 377A Challenges'. *South China Morning Post*, 30 March. www.scmp.com/week-asia/politics/article/3077581/singapore-gay-sex-still-illegal-judge-throws-out-section-377a.

Sinclair, Lian. 2020. 'Undermining Conflict: Multinational Miners, Conflict and Participation in Indonesia'. PhD, Perth: Murdoch. https://researchrepository.murdoch.edu.au/id/eprint/57011/.

Sinen, Neang. 2017. 'Thailand's Invisible Gender Law'. *Reporting ASEAN – Voices and Views from within Southeast Asia* (blog), 22 December. www.reportingasean.net/thailands-invisible-gender-law/.

Sinnott, Megan. 2004. *Toms and Dees: Transgender Identity and Female Same-Sex Relationships in Thailand*. Southeast Asia: Politics, Meaning, and Memory. Honolulu: University of Hawaii Press.

Sintos Coloma, Roland. 2013. 'Ladlad and Parrhesiastic Pedagogy: Unfurling LGBT Politics and Education in the Global South'. *Curriculum Inquiry* 43 (4): 483–511. https://doi.org/10.1111/curi.12020.

Soriano, Cheryll Ruth Reyes. 2014. 'Constructing Collectivity in Diversity: Online Political Mobilization of a National LGBT Political Party'. *Media, Culture & Society* 36 (1): 20–36.

Subpawanthanakun, Kritsada. 2017. 'Have 3 Years of the Gender Equality Act Resulted in More Equality?' *Prachatai English*, 6 December. https://prachatai.com/english/node/7503.

Sukumaran, Tashny. 2020. 'Outcry as Malaysian Minister Targets Transgender People for Arrest'. *South China Morning Post*, 17 July. www.scmp.com/week-asia/politics/article/3093482/outcry-malaysian-minister-calls-arrest-and-educate-transgender.

Sulathireh, Thilaga. 2021. Interview with Thilaga Sulathireh – Justice for Sisters.

Sutrisno, Budi. 2020. 'Activists Demand Justice for Trans Woman Burned to Death in North Jakarta'. *The Jakarta Post*, 15 April. www.thejakartapost.com/news/2020/04/14/activists-demand-justice-for-trans-woman-burned-to-death-in-north-jakarta.html.

Talabong, Rambo. 2018. 'Only 2 in 10 Filipinos Favor Same-Sex Marriage – SWS'. *Rappler*, 30 June. www.rappler.com/nation/sws-same-sex-marriage-survey-march-2018.

tan beng hui. 2019. 'The LGBT Quandary in New Malaysia'. *Australian Journal of Asian Law* 20 (1): 1–16.

tan beng hui, and Queer Lapis. 2020. '377: The Law That Changed Msia's Political History Forever'. *Malaysiakini*, 14 May. www.malaysiakini.com/news/525616.

Tan, Hsien-Li. 2011. *The Asean Intergovernmental Commission on Human Rights: Institutionalising Human Rights in Southeast Asia*. Cambridge: Cambridge University Press.

Tan, Michael L. 1995. 'Tita Aida and Emerging Communities of Gay Men'. *Journal of Gay & Lesbian Social Services* 3 (3): 31–48.

Tan, Roy. n.d.a. 'Explanatory Statement to the Maintenance of Religious Harmony Act'. *The Singapore LGBT Encyclopaedia Wiki*. https://the-singapore-lgbt-encyclopaedia.wikia.org/wiki/Explanatory_Statement_to_the_Maintenance_of_Religious_Harmony_Act.

n.d.b. 'Lee Kuan Yew's Views on Homosexuality'. *The Singapore LGBT Encyclopaedia Wiki*. https://the-singapore-lgbt-encyclopaedia.wikia.org/wiki/Lee_Kuan_Yew%27s_views_on_homosexuality.

Tee, Kenneth. 2020. 'Human Rights NGO Calls on Minister to Revoke Order for Authorities to Go after Transgender Persons in Malaysia'. *Malay Mail*, 15 July. www.malaymail.com/news/malaysia/2020/07/15/human-rights-ngo-calls-on-minister-to-revoke-order-for-authorities-to-go-af/1884834.

The Isaan Record. 2019. '"The Civil Union Bill Misses the Target" Says Thailand's First Transgender MP'. 23 May. https://isaanrecord.com/2019/05/23/the-civil-union-bill-misses-the-target/.

The Jakarta Post. 2019. 'Top Philippine Court Refuses to Legalise Gay Marriage'. 3 September. www.thejakartapost.com/seasia/2019/09/03/top-philippine-court-refuses-to-legalise-gay-marriage.html.

2020. 'House Keeps Problematic Bills in Prolegnas, Aiming to Pass Them by October'. 2 July. www.thejakartapost.com/news/2020/07/02/house-keeps-problematic-bills-in-prolegnas-aiming-to-pass-them-by-october.html.

Thomson Reuters. 2017. 'Transgender Activist Breaks Barriers to Education in Thailand'. *NBC News*, 19 January. www.nbcnews.com/feature/nbc-out/transgender-activist-breaks-barriers-education-thailand-n708366.

Thoreson, Ryan. 2020a. 'Philippines Uses Humiliation as COVID Curfew Punishment'. *Human Rights Watch*, 8 April. www.hrw.org/news/2020/04/08/philippines-uses-humiliation-covid-curfew-punishment.

2020b. 'Philippines Police Crack Down on LGBT Protest'. *Human Rights Watch*, 29 June. www.hrw.org/news/2020/06/29/philippines-police-crack-down-lgbt-protest.

TOC. 2021. 'Protest Outside Ministry of Education Reflect "Frustrations of Youths Who Are Continually Silenced": S'pore LGBT Organisations'. 26 January. www.theonlinecitizen.com/2021/01/27/protest-outside-ministry-of-education-reflect-frustrations-of-youths-who-are-continually-silenced-spore-lgbt-organisations/.

Treat, John Whittier. 2015. 'The Rise and Fall of Homonationalism in Singapore'. *Positions: Asia Critique* 23 (2): 349–65. https://doi.org/10.1215/10679847-2861026.

Tubeza, Philip C. 2017. 'Duterte Favors Same-Sex Marriage'. *Inquirer.Net*, 18 December. https://newsinfo.inquirer.net/953326/duterte-favors-same-sex-marriage.

UN. 2013. 'Ban Ki-Moon: Struggle for LGBT Right One of the Great, Neglected Human Rights Challenges of Our Time'. International Conference on Human Rights, Sexual Orientation and Gender Identity (Oslo, 15–16 April), 15 April. www.youtube.com/watch?v=7uaHZWCgGss&feature=youtube_gdata_player.

2016. 'General Assembly Adopts 50 Third Committee Resolutions, as Diverging Views on Sexual Orientation, Gender Identity Animate

Voting'. GA/11879. New York. www.un.org/press/en/2016/ga11879 .doc.htm.

UN General Assembly. 1993. 'Principles Relating to the Status of National Institutions (The Paris Principles)'. Resolution 48/134. New York.

UN HRC and SOGI Independent Expert. 2020. 'Practices of So-Called "Conversion Therapy"'. A/HRC/44/53. Geneva.

UNAIDS. 2020. 'Seizing the Moment: Tackling Entrenched Inequalities to End Epidemics'. UNAIDS/JC2991. Geneva. https://www.unaids.org/en.

UNDP. 2019. 'Tolerance but Not Inclusion: A National Survey on Experiences of Discrimination and Social Attitudes Towards LGBT People in Thailand'. Bangkok.

———. n.d. 'Being LGBTI in Asia and the Pacific'. Bangkok. www.asia-pacific.undp.org/content/rbap/en/home/programmes-and-initiatives/being-lgbt-in-asia.html.

UNDP, APF, and APCOM. 2015. 'Report of the Workshop on the Role of National Human Rights Institutions in Promoting and Protecting the Rights, Including Health, of LGBTI People in Asia and the Pacific'. Bangkok: UNDP.

UNDP and USAID. 2014. 'Being LGBT in Asia: Philippines Country Report'. Bangkok: UNDP.

Velasquez, Tony. 2015. 'Keeping It Straight: PM Says Singapore Not Ready for Gay Marriage'. *ABS-CBN News*, 27 June. https://news.abs-cbn.com/focus/06/27/15/keeping-it-straight-pm-says-singapore-not-ready-gay-marriage.

Vergara, Robert. 2019. 'SOGIE Bill "Imported," Disregarded PH Culture – Eddie Villanueva'. *CNN*, 3 September. https://cnnphilippines.com/news/2019/9/3/eddie-villanueva-sogie-equality-bill.html.

Villaruel, Jauhn Etienne. 2021. 'LGBT Groups Say Dutertes "No Ally to Us"'. *ABS-CBN News*, 7 September. https://news.abs-cbn.com/news/09/07/21/lgbt-groups-say-dutertes-no-ally-to-us.

VOI. 2020. 'Reasons for the Formation and Article of the Controversy on the Draft Family Resilience'. *Waktunya Merevolusi Pemberitaan*, 19 February. https://voi.id/en/news/2916/reasons-for-the-formation-and-article-of-the-controversy-on-the-draft-family-resilience.

Wahyuningrum, Yuyun. 2021. 'A Decade of Institutionalising Human Rights in ASEAN: Progress and Challenges'. *Journal of Human Rights* 20 (2): 158–175.

Waites, Matthew. 2009. 'Critique of "Sexual Orientation" and "Gender Identity" in Human Rights Discourse: Global Queer Politics beyond the Yogyakarta Principles'. *Contemporary Politics* 15 (1): 137–56.

Walden, Max. 2020. 'Singapore's GE2020: A Post-Mortem'. *Election Watch*, 27 August. https://electionwatch.unimelb.edu.au/articles/singapores-ge2020-a-post-mortem.

Weiss, Meredith L. 2007. '"We Know Who You Are. We'll Employ You": Non-Discrimination and Singapore's Bohemian Dreams'. In *Sexual Orientation Discrimination: An International Perspective*, edited by Mary Virginia Lee Badgett and Jeff Frank, 164–76. London: Routledge.

2013. 'Prejudice before Pride: Rise of an Anticipatory Countermovement'. In *Global Homophobia: States, Movements, and the Politics of Oppression*, edited by Meredith L. Weiss and Michael J. Bosia, 149–73. Chicago: University of Illinois Press.

2017. 'Resistance and Resilience: Coping with/against the State'. *Journal of Social Issues in Southeast Asia* 32 (2): 374–404.

2021. 'Building Solidarity on the Margins: Seeking SOGIE Rights in ASEAN'. *Journal of Human Rights* 20 (2): 194–210.

Weiss, Meredith L., and Michael J. Bosia, eds. 2013. *Global Homophobia: States, Movements, and the Politics of Oppression*. Chicago: University of Illinois Press.

Weiss, Meredith L., and Faisal S. Hazis, eds. 2020. *Towards a New Malaysia? The 2018 Election and Its Aftermath*. Singapore: National University of Singapore Press.

Wieringa, Saskia E. 2000. 'Communism and Women's Same-Sex Practises in Post-Suharto Indonesia'. *Culture, Health & Sexuality* 2 (4): 441–57.

2019. 'Criminalisation of Homosexuality in Indonesia: The Role of the Constitution and Civil Society'. *Australian Journal of Asian Law* 20 (1): 19.

Wijaya, Hendri Yulius. 2020. *Intimate Assemblages: The Politics of Queer Identities and Sexualities in Indonesia*. Singapore: Springer.

Wilson, Ian Douglas. 1999. 'Reog Ponorogo Spirituality, Sexuality, and Power in a Javanese Performance Tradition'. *Intersections: Gender and Sexuality in Asia and the Pacific*, no. 2 (May). http://intersections.anu.edu.au/issue2_contents.html.

Winter, Bronwyn. 2018. *Global Perspectives on Same-Sex Marriage*. New York: Springer Science+Business Media.

Yogyakarta Principles. 2007. 'The Yogyakarta Principles'. http://www.yogyakartaprinciples.org/.

Zivi, Karen. 2011. *Making Rights Claims: A Practice of Democratic Citizenship*. Oxford: Oxford University Press.

Zurlia, Leni. 2020. Interview with Leni Zurlia – ASEAN SOGIE Caucus.

Acknowledgements

Many thanks to Meredith Weiss for her generous editorial guidance and enthusiasm for this project; to the external reviewers for their constructive and encouraging advice; and, most critically, to the SOGIESC rights advocates throughout the region who gave their time to talk.

Allan, as always, has been stalwart in his care and support.

Cambridge Elements ☰

Politics and Society in Southeast Asia

Edward Aspinall

Australian National University

Edward Aspinall is a professor of politics at the Coral Bell School of Asia-Pacific Affairs, Australian National University. A specialist of Southeast Asia, especially Indonesia, much of his research has focused on democratisation, ethnic politics and civil society in Indonesia and, most recently, clientelism across Southeast Asia.

Meredith L. Weiss

University at Albany, SUNY

Meredith L. Weiss is Professor of Political Science at the University at Albany, SUNY. Her research addresses political mobilization and contention, the politics of identity and development, and electoral politics in Southeast Asia, with particular focus on Malaysia and Singapore.

About the Series

The Elements series Politics and Society in Southeast Asia includes both country-specific and thematic studies on one of the world's most dynamic regions. Each title, written by a leading scholar of that country or theme, combines a succinct, comprehensive, up-to-date overview of debates in the scholarly literature with original analysis and a clear argument.

Cambridge Elements ≡

Politics and Society in Southeast Asia

Elements in the Series

A full series listing is available at: www.cambridge.org/ESEA

Printed in the United States
by Baker & Taylor Publisher Services